Children's ATLAS of the World

Children's
ATLAS
of the World

Malcom Watson

Consultant: Clive Carpenter

GROLIER
In-Home Learning Expert

First published in 2007 by Miles Kelly Publishing Ltd
Harding's Barn, Bardfield End Green, Thaxted, Essex, CM6 3PX, UK

Copyright © Miles Kelly Publishing Ltd 2007

This edition updated 2013, and printed 2014

2 4 6 8 10 9 7 5 3

Author: Malcolm Watson
Consultant: Clive Carpenter

Map Artworker: Julian Baker (J B ILLUSTRATIONS)
Mountain High Maps® Copyright © 1993 Digital Wisdom, Inc.

Publishing Director: Belinda Gallagher
Creative Director: Jo Cowan
Editor: Amanda Askew
Editorial Assistant: Carly Blake
Designers: Simon Lee, Elaine Wilkinson
Cover Designer: Simon Lee
Reprographics: Stephan Davis, Jennifer Cozens,
Thom Allaway, Liberty Newton
Production: Elizabeth Collins, Caroline Kelly
Assets: Lorraine King

ISBN 978-1-78209-173-8 Hardback
ISBN 978-1-78209-151-6 Paperback

Printed in Hong Kong

British Library Cataloguing-in-Publication Data
A catalogue record for this book is available from the British Library

Made with paper from a sustainable forest

www.mileskelly.net
info@mileskelly.net

Children's ATLAS of the World

Contents

Using the atlas

Divided into continental areas, this atlas explores the world with amazing facts, statistics and photographs. Highly detailed maps show important cultural and geographical features, such as major towns, places of interest, mountain ranges and rivers.

1 Graticule
The coloured frame that runs around each map. It changes colour for each continental area and provides grid references that enable you to locate features on the map easily.

2 Main heading
Introduces the main countries on the page.

3 Locator globe
Highlights where in the world the countries are.

4 Introduction
Gives an insight into some of the countries that are mapped.

5 Scale
Shows the scale of the map in kilometres and miles.

6 Map
Shows towns, territories and islands, plus physical features such as mountain ranges.

7 Did You Know?
Amazing facts about people and places.

8 Image
Each photograph is accompanied by a detailed caption.

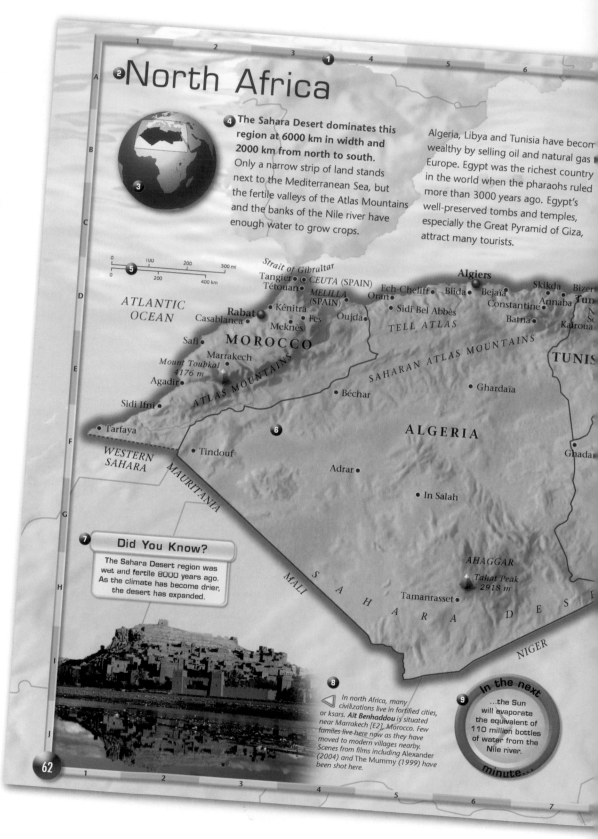

North Africa

4 The Sahara Desert dominates this region at 6000 km in width and 2000 km from north to south. Only a narrow strip of land stands next to the Mediterranean Sea, but the fertile valleys of the Atlas Mountains and the banks of the Nile river have enough water to grow crops.

Algeria, Libya and Tunisia have become wealthy by selling oil and natural gas to Europe. Egypt was the richest country in the world when the pharaohs ruled more than 3000 years ago. Egypt's well-preserved tombs and temples, especially the Great Pyramid of Giza, attract many tourists.

Did You Know?
The Sahara Desert region was wet and fertile 8000 years ago. As the climate has become drier, the desert has expanded.

In north Africa, many civilizations live in fortified cities, or ksars. **Aït Benhaddou** is situated near Marrakech [E2], Morocco. Few families live here now as they have moved to modern villages nearby. Scenes from films including Alexander (2004) and The Mummy (1999) have been shot here.

9 In the next minute... ...the Sun will evaporate the equivalent of 110 million bottles of water from the Nile river.

KEY TO MAPS

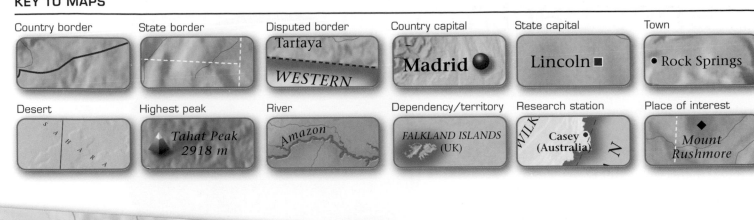

Country border	State border	Disputed border	Country capital	State capital	Town
		Tartaya / WESTERN	**Madrid** ●	Lincoln ■	● Rock Springs

Desert	Highest peak	River	Dependency/territory	Research station	Place of interest
S A H A R A	▲ Tahat Peak 2918 m	Amazon	FALKLAND ISLANDS (UK)	Casey ● (Australia)	◆ Mount Rushmore

NORTH AFRICA • AFRICA

◁ Located on the Nile river, Cairo [F13] is the biggest city in Africa. Built in AD 988, **Al-Azhar University** is the second oldest university in the world, after the University of Al Karaouine Fez, Morocco. Al-Azhar Mosque stands alongside the university.

Facts and Stats ⑭

- Egypt's population of 77.8 million would fill 778 Olympic stadiums. Libya's population of 6.4 million would only fill 64 stadiums.
- Cairo [F13] is the biggest city with 15.5 million people. This would fill 155 Olympic stadiums, compared to Tripoli which would only fill 14 [E8].
- The average income per person in Libya is £7140, compared to a world average of £5640.

Search and Find ⑩

Algeria
- Algiers C6

Egypt
- Cairo. F13

Libya
- Tripoli E8

Morocco
- Rabat D3

Tunisia
- Tunis D7

World Record ⑬
The Sahara sand sea in Algeria has the longest sand dunes in the world, with some more than 300 km.

Extreme Weather ⑮
The hottest temperature ever recorded was 58°C in Libya's Sahara Desert.

MEDITERRANEAN SEA

Tripoli
Zawiyah • Misurata
Gulf of Sidra • Benghazi • Darnah
Surt • Tubruq
• Ajdabiya
Alexandria • Tanta • Port Said
QATTARA DEPRESSION Cairo • Suez Canal
Giza • Suez
Sinai Peninsula
ISRAEL
GREAT SAND SEA Nile
ha •
LIBYA
FEZZAN
LIBYAN DESERT
WESTERN DESERT
Sharm al Sheikh
• El Minya
• Al Ghardaqah
Asyut •
Gulf of Aqaba
Gulf of Suez
RED SEA
EGYPT
• Qena
• Luxor
GILF KEBIR PLATEAU
• Aswan
Lake Nasser
CHAD
SUDAN

⑪ **THE DISTANCE** separating Morocco from Spain, Europe, at the Strait of Gibraltar's [C3] narrowest point is only 13 km.

⑫ **EGYPT** has huge pyramids, built more than 3000 years ago. Each one held the body of a king.

▷ **Desert tribe people**, such as the Berbers and Tuaregs, travel by camel from oasis to oasis across the Sahara Desert to trade cloth, salt and spices.

⑨ **In the next minute...**
Fascinating information about what is happening across the world in only one minute.

⑩ **Search and Find**
Each country or state is listed with its capital city and a grid reference.

⑪ **The distance...**
Measures the distance from one point to another and how long it would take to travel.

⑫ **Place of interest**
Provides extra information about a well-known sight or attraction.

⑬ **World Record**
Details a world record that a country holds.

⑭ **Facts and Stats**
Helps you to understand facts and figures. The highest peaks are compared to the Eiffel Tower in Paris, France, which is 320 m in height. Rivers are compared to the Nile river, Africa, which is 6670 km in length. Population is compared to an Olympic stadium, which would hold 100,000 people.

⑮ **Extreme Weather**
Details the highest and lowest temperatures, dramatic storms or high rainfall.

63

Planet Earth

Earth is a huge ball of rock with two-thirds of its surface covered by seas and oceans. The third planet from the Sun in the Solar System, Earth is the only planet where life is known to exist, due to an atmosphere rich in oxygen and the water on its surface. Beneath the Earth's thin, solid crust is the liquid mantle, and at the centre is the core. The outer part of the core is liquid, but the inner core is solid metal.

Continental crust
0–50 km

Lithosphere, asthenosphere and mesosphere 0–400 km

Mantle
10–2890 km

Core
Outer – 2890–5150 km
Inner – below 5150 km

▲ There are three main parts to the Earth – the crust, mantle and core. Although the inner core reaches a temperature of 7000°C, it remains solid because the pressure is 6000 times greater than on the surface.

SPINNING EARTH

The Earth spins on its axis – an imaginary line through its centre – at a speed of more than 1600 km/h. It doesn't spin straight up, but leans to one side. As the Earth spins, the view of the Sun from different places on Earth constantly changes. This brings day and night, and the seasons.

▼ In December, the South Pole leans towards the Sun. Places in the southern half of the world have summer. At the same time, places in the northern half have winter.

Seasons
There are four seasons – spring, summer, autumn and winter. Each season brings a change in temperature and weather. The changes in the seasons occur because the Earth tilts towards the Sun. When the Northern Hemisphere tilts towards the Sun, the northern part of the world has summer and the south has winter. Six months later, the opposite occurs – the Southern Hemisphere tilts towards the Sun. Then the north has winter and the south has summer. The tropics around the centre of the Earth are slightly different. They only have two seasons – wet and dry.

Northern Hemisphere is tilted away from the Sun – winter

Sun

Southern Hemisphere is tilted towards the Sun – summer

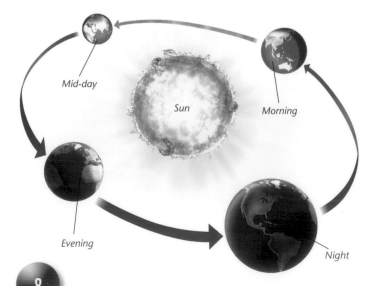

Mid-day

Sun

Morning

Evening

Night

◀ When it is daylight on the half of the Earth facing towards the Sun, it is night on the half of the Earth facing away from it. As the Earth rotates, so the day and night halves shift gradually around the world.

Night and day
The Earth spins a complete turn on its axis every 24 hours. This gives us night and day. The Sun is the source of light for daytime. When it is night, it is dark because the Sun is shining on the opposite side of the Earth. When it is evening or early morning, the Sun is moving away or towards our part of the Earth.

Shaping the land

The Earth's crust is made up of pieces called tectonic plates, which are constantly moving, changing the shape of the land. This can create mountains and volcanoes, as well as cause natural disasters, such as earthquakes. Rocks can also be broken down or worn away by the weather, such as wind and rain, or by the movement of water, such as waves.

A volcano erupts, shooting molten magma into the air.

A sea arch, formed by waves wearing away the rock.

PLATE TECTONICS

The Earth's crust is split into several parts called tectonic plates. The plates float on the molten magma underneath, causing them to constantly move.

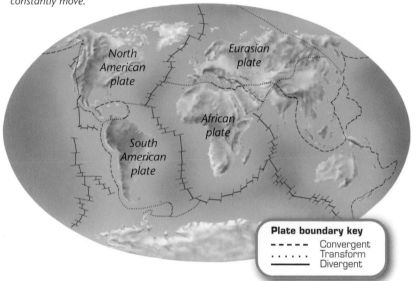

North American plate

Eurasian plate

African plate

South American plate

Plate boundary key

- - - - - Convergent
. . . . . . Transform
———— Divergent

Divergent plate boundaries

Where two plates move away from each other, molten rock, or magma, rises to fill the gap. This usually occurs beneath the oceans, forming a spreading ocean ridge, such as the mid-Atlantic ridge.

Mid-ocean ridge

Plates move apart

Ocean plate

Magma erupts through the gap

Mantle

Convergent plate boundaries

When two plates crash together, they crumple up and form major mountain chains, such as the Andes, as well as volcanoes. The Earth's crust is thin, so if cracks appear, the magma shoots up as the lava of a volcano. When an ocean plate is driven down into the Earth's magma, it is called subduction.

Plates move together

Ocean trench

Continental crust

Subducted ocean trench bends down

Continental lithosphere

Mantle

Subducted plate melting into magma

Volcano along the edge of the overlying plate

Mountain range forms

Transform plate boundaries

If two plates push past each other, pressure can build up, creating a break, or fault, which often causes an earthquake. Some earthquakes are so powerful that buildings collapse. Landslides can also occur, causing great damage. Undersea earthquakes can cause the massive waves of a tsunami, such as the tsunami that struck southeast Asia in 2004, killing 230,000 people.

Plates push past each other

Mantle

Climate

The Earth's climate is very simple. Near the Equator, the temperture is hot, and closer to the poles, the temperature is cold. All year round, daytime tempertures at the Equator are around 33°C and there are no seasons. At the poles, the temperature is usually below freezing, and in winter there are long hours of darkness and temperatures drop to −40°C. Rain and snowfall patterns are more complex. Countries at the Equator experience heavy rain, but the poles have very little rainfall.

Global warming

The increased level of carbon dioxide in the atmosphere causes global warming because the gas traps the Sun's heat. Carbon dioxide is emitted when carbon fuels are burnt – this happens in cars and factories. The effects of global warming are becoming evident. Large areas of ice around Antarctica have already disappeared. The Sahara Desert is expanding and droughts are more common in Australia, causing rivers, such as the Murray, to dry up (see below). Sea levels are slowly rising, threatening cities such as New York City and low-lying countries such as Bangladesh with flooding. Using alternative sources of energy, such as wind and solar power, is vital to slow down these changes.

TYPES OF CLIMATE

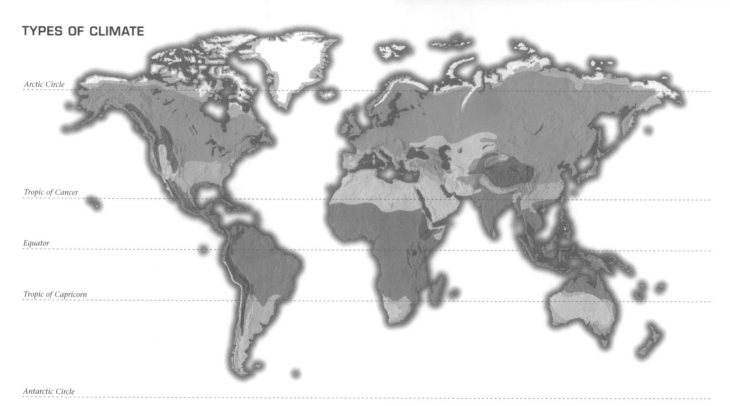

Arctic Circle

Tropic of Cancer

Equator

Tropic of Capricorn

Antarctic Circle

Polar and tundra
The lands around the Arctic Ocean and Antarctica are normally covered in snow. Northern Canada and Russia have a brief summer where the snow melts and the top layer of soil thaws to create a boggy ground called tundra.

Desert
Just north and south of the Equator lie desert areas. They have high daytime summer temperatures and are warm even in winter. Rain is very rare. Few plants grow and crops are only farmed where there are sources of water.

Cool temperate
Near the Arctic Circle, winters are cold and snowy, and summers are short. Closer to the Equator winters are milder, with little snow and warm summers. Forests are abundant and farming is common in the southern areas.

Warm temperate
In areas around the Mediterranean Sea and in some parts of North America, summers are hot and dry and winters are cool, but mild. Rainfall varies, so farming centres around growing citrus and olive trees.

Tropical
Close to the Equator, countries experience high temperatures and high rainfall for almost every month of the year. More animals and plants live in the tropical rainforests of the Amazon, central Africa and Indonesia than any other region.

Mountainous
Mountains have their own climate and snow can even be found at the Equator. At 5000 m in height, the temperature is 30°C colder than at sea level. Mountains also have more rainfall than the land surrounding them.

Population

The population of the world reached 6.7 billion in 2008. With more than 250 babies being born each minute, and many people living longer due to a better quality of life, the population of the world is increasing rapidly. This rise puts pressure on the world's natural resources, and many cities are becoming overcrowded as people move in search of work. China is the most populated country with 1.24 billion people. Tokyo, the capital of Japan, is the largest city in the world with a population of 37.36 million.

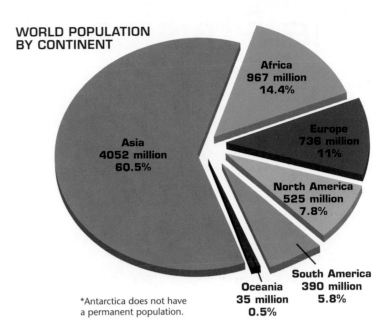

WORLD POPULATION BY CONTINENT

Asia 4052 million 60.5%

Africa 967 million 14.4%

Europe 736 million 11%

North America 525 million 7.8%

South America 390 million 5.8%

Oceania 35 million 0.5%

*Antarctica does not have a permanent population.

TOP 10 COUNTRIES BY POPULATION DENSITY

Country	People per km²
Monaco	15,550
Singapore	6433
Malta	1297
Vatican City	1272
Bahrain	1012
Maldives	1003
Bangladesh	875
Barbados	632
Mauritius	612
San Marino	504

People per km² 0   5000   10,000   15,000   20,000

TOP 10 COUNTRIES BY POPULATION

1	China	1,240,000,000
2	India	1,148,000,000
3	USA	304,060,000
4	Indonesia	222,192,000
5	Brazil	183,889,000
6	Pakistan	162,508,000
7	Russia	142,754,000
8	Nigeria	140,003,000
9	Bangladesh	129,247,000
10	Japan	127,931,000

TOP 20 CITIES BY POPULATION

1 Tokyo 37,360,000	6 Osaka 17,600,000	11 Delhi 12,791,000	16 Tehran 11,850,000
2 Seoul 21,300,000	7 Mumbai (Bombay) 16,368,000	12 Istanbul 12,574,000	17 Rio De Janeiro 11,563,000
3 Mexico City 19,232,000	8 Jakarta 13,660,000	13 Moscow 12,400,000	18 Dhaka 10,404,000
4 São Paulo 19,226,000	9 Kolkata (Calcutta) 13,217,000	14 Cairo 12,200,000	19 Paris 10,143,000
5 New York City 19,007,000	10 Los Angeles 12,873,000	15 Buenos Aires 12,047,000	20 Shanghai 9,838,000

The Physical World

QUEEN ELIZABETH ISLANDS

Ellesmere Island

GREENLAND (DENMARK)

BEAUFORT SEA

Victoria Island

Baffin Bay

Baffin Island

NORWEGIAN SEA

BROOKS RANGE

Great Bear Lake

Back

Little Bear Lake

Mackenzie

Yukon

Gulf of Alaska

ROCKY MOUNTAINS

GREAT PLAINS

HUDSON BAY

CANADIAN SHIELD

Davis Strait

Denmark Strait

NO S

ALEUTIAN ISLANDS

Lake Winnipeg

Missouri

Mississippi

THE GREAT LAKES

CANADIAN SHIELD

Newfoundland

MID-ATLANTIC RIDGE

PACIFIC OCEAN

NORTH AMERICA

NORTH ATLANTIC OCEAN

CANARY ISLANDS (SPAIN)

ATLAS MOUNTAINS

Hawaii (US)

Rio Grande

SIERRA MADRE

GULF OF MEXICO

SAHARA

MID-AMERICA TRENCH

WEST INDIES

CARIBBEAN SEA

Niger

Galápagos Islands (Ecuador)

LLANOS

Orinoco

GUIANA HIGHLANDS

GULF OF GUINEA

MID-ATLANTIC RIDGE

ANDES

Amazon

SOUTH AMERICA

SOUTH ATLANTIC OCEAN

SELVAS

BRAZILIAN HIGHLANDS

PERU-CHILE TRENCH

GRAN CHACO

PAMPAS

WALVIS R

FALKLAND ISLANDS (UK)

Cape Horn

Antarctic

LONGEST RIVERS BY CONTINENT

River	Continent	Length km
Nile	Africa	6670
Chang Jiang (Yangze)	Asia	6300
Volga	Europe	3530
Mississippi-Missouri	North America	6020

LOWEST POINTS BY CONTINENT

Area	Continent	Depth m
Lake Assal	Africa	−153
Dead Sea	Asia	−402
Caspian Sea shore	Europe	−28
Death Valley	North America	−86
Lake Eyre	Oceania	−16

HIGHEST POINTS BY CONTINENT

Mountain	Continent	Height m
Mount Kilimanjaro	Africa	5895
Mount Everest	Asia	8848
Mount Elbrus	Europe	5642
Mount McKinley	North America	6194
Puncak Jaya	Oceania	5030

| 0 | 1000 | 2000 | 3000 mi |
| 0 | 1000 | 2000 | 3000 | 4000 | 5000 km |

OCEAN

Franz Josef Land

Severnaya Zemlya

SVALBARD
(NORWAY)

Novaya Zemlya

KARA
SEA

LAPTEV SEA

NEW SIBERIAN
ISLANDS

EAST
SIBERIAN
SEA

BARENTS
SEA

LAPLAND

URAL MOUNTAINS

Dvina

CENTRAL
SIBERIAN
PLATEAU

Lena

BALTIC SEA

Ob

SIBERIAN
LOWLAND

Yenisey

Nizhnyaya Tunguska

BERING
SEA

TH EUROPEAN PLAIN

Volga

Ob

Yenisey

Lena

Aldan

EUROPE

URAL MOUNTAINS

Ural

Angara

ASIA

Lake
Baikal

SEA OF
OKHOTSK

CARPATHIAN
MOUNTAINS

Dnieper

Irtysh

SAYAN MOUNTAINS

GOBI
DESERT

KURIL TRENCH

Danube

BLACK SEA

CASPIAN SEA

Aral
Sea

Lake
Balkhash

MEDITERRANEAN SEA

ZAGROS MOUNTAINS

Euphrates

Tigris

TIEN MOUNTAINS

HINDU KUSH

KUNLUN MOUNTAINS

TIBETAN
PLATEAU

Indus

HIMALAYAS

Huang

Chang Jiang

SEA OF
JAPAN

DESERT

Nile

RED SEA

Arabian
Peninsula

ARABIAN
SEA

Ganges

DECCAN

Irrawaddy

EAST CHINA
SEA

PACIFIC
OCEAN

NUBIAN
DESERT

GULF OF ADEN

BAY OF
BENGAL

Mekong

SOUTH
CHINA
SEA

MICRONESIA

FRICA

Uele

ETHIOPIAN
HIGHLANDS

MID-INDIAN RIDGE

PHILIPPINE SEA

Congo

GREAT RIFT VALLEY

Lake
Victoria

CELEBES
SEA

MELANESIA

CONGO
BASIN

Kasai

EAST INDIES

Orange

JAVA TRENCH

INDIAN
OCEAN

CORAL
SEA

KALAHARI
DESERT

GREAT SANDY
DESERT

GREAT DIVIDING RANGE

OCEANIA

SOUTHEAST INDIAN RIDGE

GREAT
VICTORIAN
DESERT

Cape of
Good Hope

SOUTHWEST INDIAN RIDGE

SOUTHERN
OCEAN

Great
Australian
Bight

TASMAN
SEA

WORLD'S OCEANS	
Ocean	**Area km²**
Pacific	165,240,000
Atlantic	82,440,000
Indian	73,440,000
Southern	23,325,000
Arctic	14,090,000

LARGEST DESERTS		
Desert	**Continent**	**Area km²**
Sahara	Africa	8,600,000
Arabian	Asia	2,300,000
Australian	Australia	1,550,000
Gobi	Asia	1,300,000
Kalahari	Africa	930,000

LARGEST INLAND WATER BODIES		
Lake	**Continent**	**Area km²**
Caspian Sea	Asia–Europe	371,800
Superior	North America	82,350
Victoria	Africa	69,500
Huron	North America	59,600
Michigan	North America	57,800

ARCTIC OCEAN

FINLAND
WAY
SWEDEN
ESTONIA
MARK
LATVIA
23   24
28
BELARUS
POLAND
29   30
35   UKRAINE
6   34   33   31
37   32
38   39   40
45   41 42   BULGARIA   GEORGIA
46   44   43
ITALY
ARMENIA   AZERBAIJAN
GREECE   TURKEY
49
CYPRUS   SYRIA
NISIA   LEBANON   IRAQ   IRAN
ISRAEL
JORDAN   KUWAIT
LIBYA   EGYPT   BAHRAIN   QATAR
SAUDI   UNITED
ARABIA   ARAB
EMIRATES
GER   CHAD   OMAN
SUDAN   ERITREA   YEMEN
ERIA   DJIBOUTI
CENTRAL   SOUTH
AFRICAN   SUDAN ETHIOPIA
REPUBLIC
AMEROON
50   KENYA
DEMOCRATIC   UGANDA
GABON   REPUBLIC
OF THE CONGO
52   RWANDA
3   BURUNDI   TANZANIA
SEYCHELLES
ANGOLA
COMOROS
ZAMBIA   MALAWI   MAYOTTE
(FRANCE)
MOZAMBIQUE
NAMIBIA   ZIMBABWE   MADAGASCAR   MAURITIUS
BOTSWANA   RÉUNION
(FRANCE)
SWAZILAND
SOUTH   LESOTHO
AFRICA

RUSSIAN FEDERATION

KAZAKHSTAN
MONGOLIA

UZBEKISTAN
KYRGYZSTAN
TURKMENISTAN
TAJIKISTAN
NORTH
KOREA
AFGHANISTAN
CHINA
SOUTH   JAPAN
KOREA

PAKISTAN
NEPAL   BHUTAN
BANGLADESH
INDIA   TAIWAN
BURMA
(MYANMAR)   LAOS
THAILAND
VIETNAM
CAMBODIA
SRI
LANKA   PHILIPPINES
MALDIVES
BRUNEI
MALAYSIA
SINGAPORE

INDONESIA
PAPUA
NEW
GUINEA
EAST
TIMOR

CORAL SEA
ISLANDS TERRITORY
(AUSTRALIA)

AUSTRALIA

NEW CALEDONIA
(FRANCE)

NEW
ZEALAND

PACIFIC
OCEAN

MARSHALL
ISLANDS

MICRONESIA
AND PALAU

NAURU
KIRIBATI

TUVALU

SAMOA

VANUATU   FIJI

TONGA

INDIAN
OCEAN

SOUTHERN OCEAN

Scale:
0   1000   2000   3000 mi
0   1000   2000   3000   4000   5000 km

MOST WIDELY SPOKEN LANGUAGES	
Language	**Number of native speakers**
Chinese Mandarin	875 million
Hindi	350 million
Spanish	340 million
English	320 million
Arabic	210 million
Bengali	210 million
Portuguese	175 million
Russian	145 million
Japanese	128 million
French	100 million

RCTICA

Antarctica

Antarctica is 98 percent covered by ice that is about 1.6 km thick. Although it is the coldest place on Earth, the region is heavily affected by global warming. The climate is becoming warmer due to an increased level of carbon dioxide, which traps the Sun's heat. Large areas of ice that cover the sea around Antarctica have already broken away and melted. Deep under the ice lie vast amounts of oil, coal and gold, but mining is prohibited.

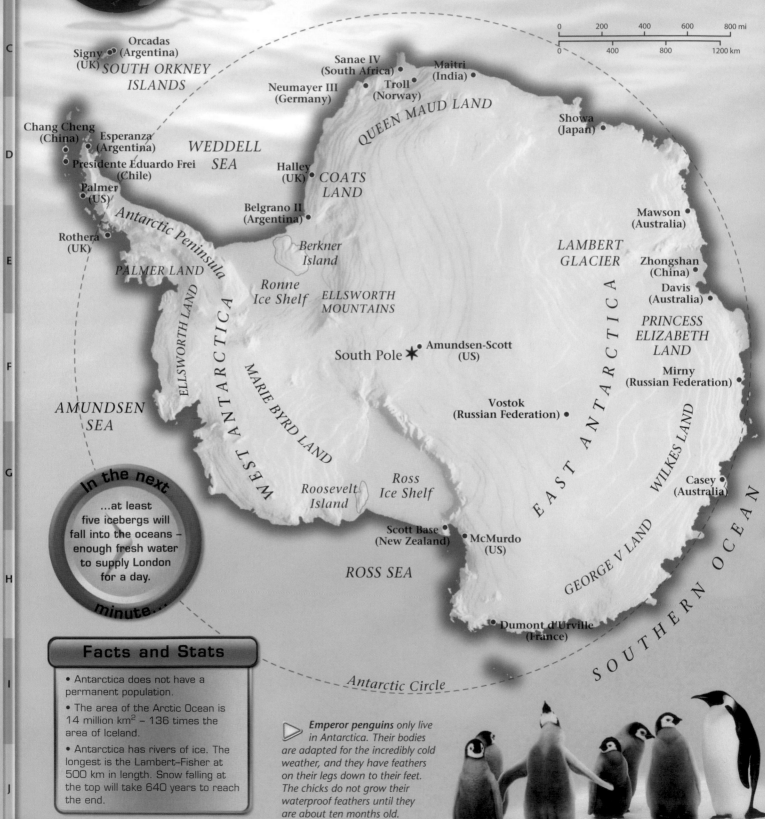

| 0 | 200 | 400 | 600 | 800 mi |
| 0 | 400 | 800 | 1200 km |

Orcadas (Argentina)
Signy (UK)
SOUTH ORKNEY ISLANDS

Sanae IV (South Africa)
Maitri (India)
Neumayer III (Germany)
Troll (Norway)
QUEEN MAUD LAND
Showa (Japan)

Chang Cheng (China)
Esperanza (Argentina)
WEDDELL SEA
Presidente Eduardo Frei (Chile)
Palmer (US)
Halley (UK)
COATS LAND
Belgrano II (Argentina)
Mawson (Australia)
LAMBERT GLACIER
Zhongshan (China)
Davis (Australia)

Antarctic Peninsula
Rothera (UK)
Berkner Island
PALMER LAND
Ronne Ice Shelf
ELLSWORTH MOUNTAINS
PRINCESS ELIZABETH LAND

ELLSWORTH LAND
AMUNDSEN SEA
WEST ANTARCTICA
MARIE BYRD LAND
South Pole ✳ Amundsen-Scott (US)
EAST ANTARCTICA
Mirny (Russian Federation)
Vostok (Russian Federation)

Ross Ice Shelf
Roosevelt Island
WILKES LAND
Casey (Australia)

Scott Base (New Zealand)
McMurdo (US)
GEORGE V LAND
SOUTHERN OCEAN
ROSS SEA

Dumont d'Urville (France)

Antarctic Circle

In the next ...at least five icebergs will fall into the oceans – enough fresh water to supply London for a day. minute...

Facts and Stats

- Antarctica does not have a permanent population.
- The area of the Arctic Ocean is 14 million km² – 136 times the area of Iceland.
- Antarctica has rivers of ice. The longest is the Lambert–Fisher at 500 km in length. Snow falling at the top will take 640 years to reach the end.

▷ *Emperor penguins only live in Antarctica. Their bodies are adapted for the incredibly cold weather, and they have feathers on their legs down to their feet. The chicks do not grow their waterproof feathers until they are about ten months old.*

Arctic Ocean

The Arctic is actually an ocean, not an area of land. Explorers have walked to the North Pole in spring when the ice is thickest, and a submarine once surfaced through the ice in late summer. The ice covering the Arctic Ocean is getting thinner and less extensive each year due to the effect of global warming – an increase in the temperature of the Earth's atmosphere. As a result, many animals, including polar bears, could eventually die out.

CHUKCHI SEA

Point Barrow

BEAUFORT SEA

Amundsen Gulf

EAST SIBERIAN SEA

Novosibirskiye Ostrova

Banks Island

LAPTEV SEA

Victoria Island

Melville Island

ARCTIC OCEAN

QUEEN ELIZABETH ISLANDS

Severnaya Zemlya

North Pole ✳

Ellesmere Island

Nares Strait   LINCOLN SEA

Baffin Island

Kap Morris Jesup   WANDEL SEA

Franz Josef Land

Novaya Zemlya

Baffin Bay

GREENLAND SEA

SVALBARD (NORWAY)

BARENTS SEA

KARA SEA

GREENLAND (DENMARK)

0	200	400	600	800 mi
0	400	800	1200 km	

Did You Know?

In Antarctica, the lowest temperature ever recorded was −89.6°C. The average summer temperature is −30°C – just 10°C warmer than a deep freezer.

NORWEGIAN SEA

THE DISTANCE from the North Pole [F11] to the South Pole [F4] is 19,996 km and would take 28 hours to travel by plane.

Arctic Circle

North America

ARCTIC OCEAN

Alaska
(US)

CANADA

PACIFIC
OCEAN

UNITED STATES
OF AMERICA

ATLANTIC
OCEAN

MEXICO

Hawaii
(US)

COUNTRY FACTFILE

Country	Life expectancy	Population in thousands	Population growth %	Population as urban %	Literacy %	Area km²	Population density per km²	Capital city	Currency	Languages
Canada	81	33,477	0.8	82	99	9,970,610	3.4	Ottawa	Canadian Dollar	English, French
Mexico	77	112,338	1.1	78	86	1,958,201	57.4	Mexico City	Mexican Peso	Spanish
United States of America	78	308,467	0.9	82	99	9,629,091	31.9	Washington D.C.	US Dollar	English, Spanish

NB: Central America can be found as part of the South and Central America section.

Northeast USA

The northeast is the centre of the United States' industry and commerce with many large manufacturing companies. Ford and General Motor vehicles, as well as coal mines, steel works, the New York Stock Exchange, Washington White House and the Senate buildings are all situated here. Modern black music started in Cleveland and Detroit, whilst away from the cities there are many beaches, rivers, forests and lakes.

Lake of the Woods

Isle Royale

Lake Superior

CANADA

Red Lake

NORTH DAKOTA

Marquette

Upper Peninsula

Moorhead

Duluth

MICHIGAN

MINNESOTA

WISCONSIN

Green Bay

Lower Peninsula

SOUTH DAKOTA

Minnesota

Minneapolis
Bloomington
Burnsville

St. Paul

Eau Claire

Green Bay
Appleton
Oshkosh

Lake Winnebago

Lake Michigan

Saginaw

Flin

Mankato

Rochester

La Crosse

Grand Rapids

Lansing

Wisconsin

Waukesha

Madison
Janesville

Milwaukee

Ann Arbo
Kalamazoo

Mason City

Cedar

Rockford

Elgin

South Bend

Waterloo

Sioux City

IOWA

Cedar Rapids
Davenport

Aurora
Joliet

Chicago
Gary

Fort Wayne

Des Moines

Council Bluffs

NEBRASKA

Des Moines

ILLINOIS

Wabash

INDIANA

Peoria

Munci

Illinois

MISSOURI

Champaign

Anderson

Decatur

Terre Haute

Indianapo

Springfield

Mississippi

Bloomington

Jeffersonville

East St. Louis

Evansville

There are 30 major league baseball teams in two leagues, the American League (founded 1901) and the National League (founded 1876).1903 was the first time that the World Series, between the winners of the two leagues, was played.

Search and Find

- Washington D.C.
  . . . . H11
Connecticut
- Hartford F12
Delaware
- Dover G11
Illinois
- Springfield. I5
Indiana
- Indianapolis . . H7
Iowa
- Des Moines . . . G3
Maine
- Augusta D13
Maryland
- Annapolis . . . H11
Massachusetts
- Boston E13
Michigan
- Lansing F7

Minnesota
- St. Paul E3
New Hampshire
- Concord E13
New Jersey
- Trenton G12
New York
- Albany E12
Ohio
- Columbus H8
Pennsylvania
- Harrisburg . . G11
Rhode Island
- Providence . . E13
Vermont
- Montpelier. . . D12
West Virginia
- Charleston I9
Wisconsin
- Madison F5

Facts and Stats

- The biggest city is New York City [F12] with 19 million people. This would fill 190 Olympic stadiums.
- The biggest lake is Lake Superior [C5] at 82,350 km², This is only 20 percent smaller than Iceland.
- Mount Washington [D12] is the highest mountain at 1917 m – six times higher than the Eiffel Tower.

Scale:
0   50   100   150   200 mi
0   100   200   300 km

Did You Know?

The five Great Lakes between USA and Canada are Michigan, Superior, Ontario, Huron and Erie. They contain one-fifth of the world's fresh water – 22.8 quadrillion litres.

In the next ...204 million litres of water will crash over Niagara Falls [F9] – enough for one million baths. **minute...**

THE DISTANCE from New York City [F12] to London across the Atlantic Ocean is 4800 km and would take seven hours by plane.

THE STATUE OF LIBERTY Island [F12], was made in and shipped to USA in are 354 steps leading to the top.

Map labels:
Presque Isle
MAINE
Penobscot
Bangor
Newport
Augusta
Lewiston
Gulf of Maine
Mount Washington 1917 m
Burlington
VERMONT
Montpelier
NEW HAMPSHIRE
Portland
Concord
Portsmouth
Manchester
Lowell
Watertown
ADIRONDACK MOUNTAINS
MASSACHUSETTS
Boston
Cape Cod
CANADA
Worcester
Springfield
NEW YORK
Providence
Lake Ontario
Utica
Schenectady
Troy
RHODE ISLAND
Syracuse
Albany
CONNECTICUT
Rochester
Hartford
Niagara Falls
New Haven
Buffalo
Bridgeport
Lake Huron
Stamford
Long Island
Port Huron
Scranton
Paterson
New York City
Susquehanna
Newark
ATLANTIC OCEAN
Warren
Erie
Ellis Island
Detroit
Lake Erie
Allegheny
Allentown
NEW JERSEY
Jersey City
Toledo
Reading
Cleveland
PENNSYLVANIA
Trenton
Akron
Harrisburg
Philadelphia
Canton
Youngstown
Vineland
Atlantic City
Pittsburgh
Wilmington
OHIO
Dover
Wheeling
Baltimore
DELAWARE
Columbus
Morgantown
MARYLAND
Annapolis
Dayton
Washington D.C.
Kettering
WEST VIRGINIA
APPALACHIAN MOUNTAINS
ncinnati
Charleston
KENTUCKY
Huntington
VIRGINIA

21

Southeast USA

The warm climate of Florida and the Gulf of Mexico coastal areas makes southeast USA popular with tourists. There is Disney World in Florida for fun, Cape Canaveral for space rocket launches, Miami for beaches, New Orleans for jazz, Nashville for country music and the Mississippi river for boat trips. Farming is the main occupation – mainly of tobacco, oranges, rice, peanuts, vegetables and cotton. There are many oil and gas rigs in the Gulf of Mexico to generate energy resources.

GRACELAND, Nashville [C8], is the home of Elvis Presley (1935–1977) and is visited by more than 600,000 fans a year.

THE DISTANCE from the source to the mouth of the Mississippi–Missouri river is 6020 km and would take 20 days floating on a raft.

Extreme Weather

Hurricane Katrina, the largest hurricane ever recorded in the USA, caused 80 percent of New Orleans [H6] to flood. More than one million people were evacuated and 1833 died.

The **Kentucky Derby** takes place in Louisville [B8] on the first Saturday of May. The race is 2 km in length and more than 150,000 spectators attend the two-week-long festival every year.

World Record

The largest space rocket launch site in the world is at Cape Canaveral [H11].

IOWA
ILLINOIS
St. Joseph
Independence
Kansas City
Columbia
Jefferson City
St. Louis
Owensboro
KANSAS
MISSOURI
Cape Girardeau
Paducah
Springfield
Clarksville
OZARK PLATEAU
OKLAHOMA
ARKANSAS
Memphis
Fort Smith
Little Rock
Mississippi
Yazoo
Hot Springs
Pine Bluff
Ouachita
Greenville
Tuscaloos
Texarkana
El Dorado
MISSISSIPPI
Monroe
Meridian
TEXAS
Shreveport
Jackson
Pearl
LOUISIANA
Natchez
Hattiesburg
Red
Alexandria
Prichard
Mobil
Biloxi
Baton Rouge
Lafayette
Metairie
New Orleans
Lake Charles
Marsh Island
Mississippi Delta

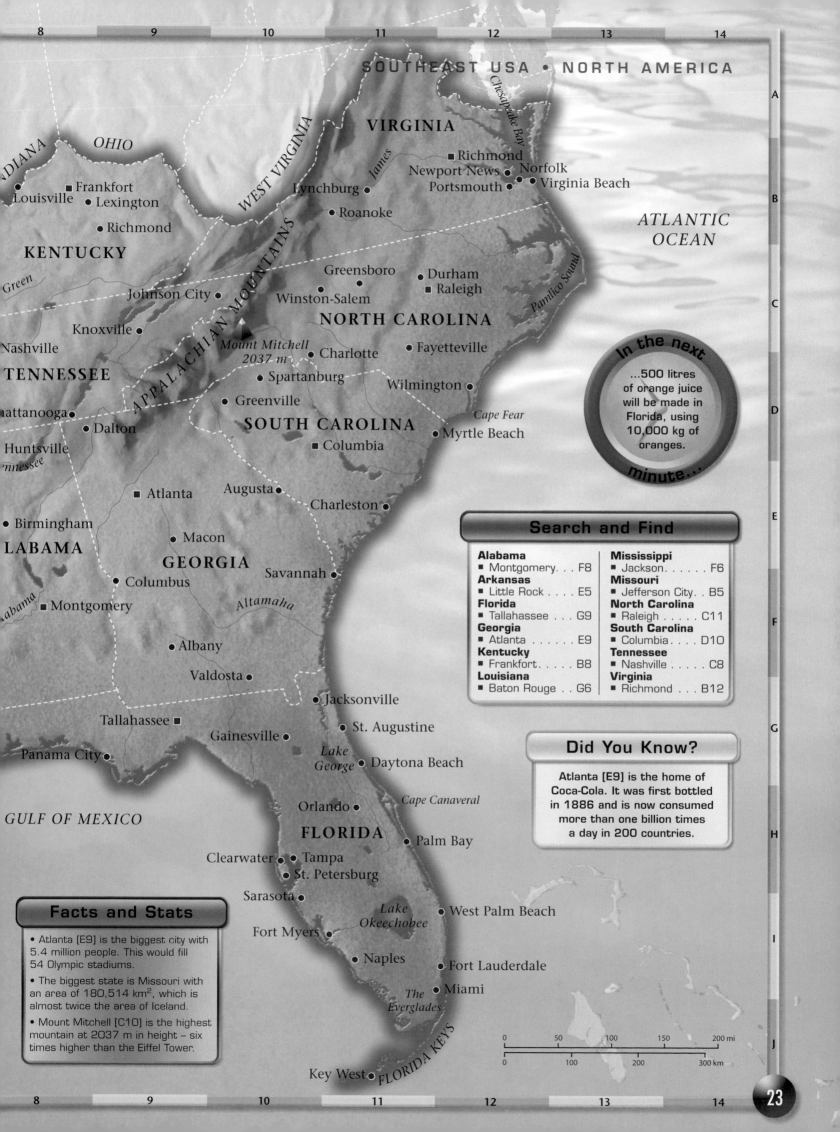

VIRGINIA

■ Richmond
Newport News ● ● Norfolk
Portsmouth ● ● Virginia Beach
Lynchburg ●

● Roanoke

ATLANTIC OCEAN

James

Chesapeake Bay

INDIANA
OHIO

● Frankfort
Louisville ● ● Lexington

● Richmond

KENTUCKY

Green

WEST VIRGINIA

Johnson City ●

Greensboro ● ● Durham
Winston-Salem ● ● Raleigh

Pamlico Sound

Knoxville ●

Nashville ●

NORTH CAROLINA

APPALACHIAN MOUNTAINS

TENNESSEE

Mount Mitchell 2037 m ● Charlotte ● Fayetteville

Chattanooga ●
● Dalton ● Spartanburg Wilmington ●

Huntsville ●
Tennessee

● Greenville

SOUTH CAROLINA

Cape Fear

● Myrtle Beach

● Birmingham

ALABAMA

■ Atlanta Augusta ● ● Columbia

Charleston ●

● Macon

GEORGIA

Savannah ●

● Columbus

Alabama

■ Montgomery

Altamaha

● Albany

Valdosta ●

Tallahassee ■

● Jacksonville

● St. Augustine

Gainesville ●

Lake George

● Daytona Beach

Panama City ●

GULF OF MEXICO

Orlando ●

Cape Canaveral

FLORIDA

● Palm Bay

Clearwater ● ● Tampa
● St. Petersburg

Sarasota ●

Lake Okeechobee

● West Palm Beach

Fort Myers ●

● Naples

● Fort Lauderdale

The Everglades

● Miami

Key West ● *FLORIDA KEYS*

In the next
...500 litres of orange juice will be made in Florida, using 10,000 kg of oranges.
minute...

Search and Find

Alabama
■ Montgomery... F8
Arkansas
■ Little Rock E5
Florida
■ Tallahassee ... G9
Georgia
■ Atlanta E9
Kentucky
■ Frankfort..... B8
Louisiana
■ Baton Rouge .. G6

Mississippi
■ Jackson...... F6
Missouri
■ Jefferson City.. B5
North Carolina
■ Raleigh C11
South Carolina
■ Columbia ... D10
Tennessee
■ Nashville C8
Virginia
■ Richmond ... B12

Did You Know?

Atlanta [E9] is the home of Coca-Cola. It was first bottled in 1886 and is now consumed more than one billion times a day in 200 countries.

Facts and Stats

• Atlanta [E9] is the biggest city with 5.4 million people. This would fill 54 Olympic stadiums.

• The biggest state is Missouri with an area of 180,514 km², which is almost twice the area of Iceland.

• Mount Mitchell [C10] is the highest mountain at 2037 m in height – six times higher than the Eiffel Tower.

0 50 100 150 200 mi
0 100 200 300 km

Northwest USA and Alaska

Inland areas in northwest USA are **either stunning mountain scenery or vast ranches.** Washington's Seattle is the only large urban area, with the Boeing aircraft factory, and the headquarters of Microsoft, UPS, Starbucks and Amazon. The USA's biggest apple-growing region stretches from the Pacific Ocean to the Great Plains of the Dakotas. Alaska is the USA's largest state. However, vast areas are uninhabited due to long, severe winters. Alaska is one of the leading oil-producing regions in the world.

In the next
...Wyoming will produce 300 tonnes of coal – enough to produce electricity to power ten million TVs.
minute...

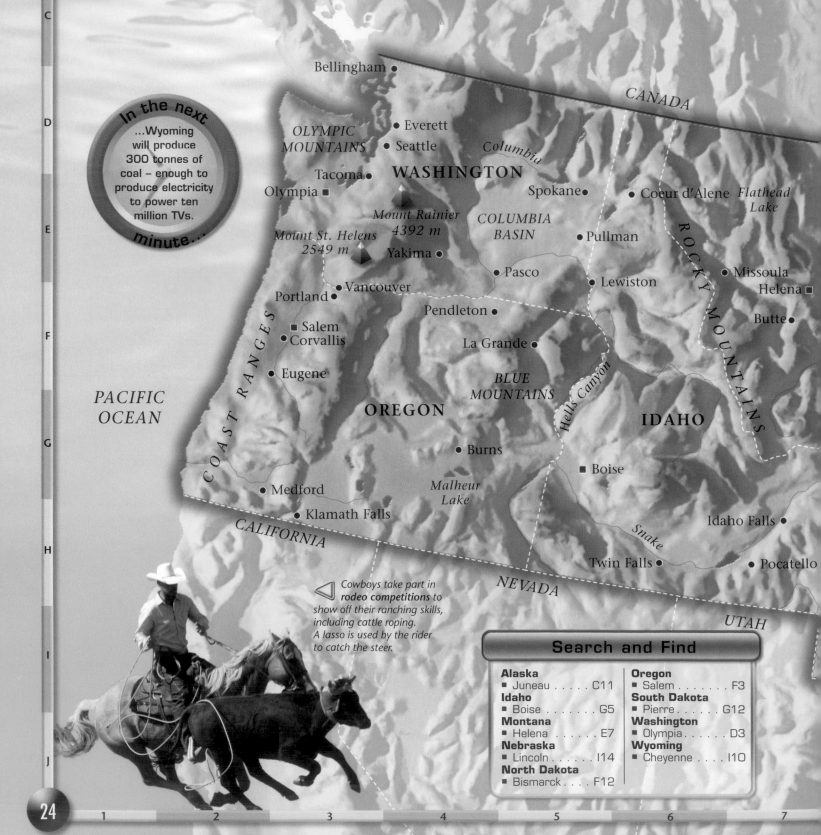

CANADA

Bellingham

OLYMPIC MOUNTAINS

Everett
Seattle

Columbia

Tacoma
WASHINGTON

Olympia ■
Spokane
Coeur d'Alene   *Flathead Lake*

Mount Rainier 4392 m

COLUMBIA BASIN

R O C K Y   M O U N T A I N S

Mount St. Helens 2549 m
Yakima
Pullman

Pasco
Lewiston
Missoula
Helena ■

Portland
Vancouver

Salem
Corvallis

Pendleton
Butte

La Grande

C O A S T   R A N G E S

Eugene

BLUE MOUNTAINS

Hells Canyon

OREGON

IDAHO

PACIFIC OCEAN

Burns

Boise

Medford

Malheur Lake

Klamath Falls

CALIFORNIA

Snake

Idaho Falls

NEVADA

Twin Falls
Pocatello

UTAH

Cowboys take part in **rodeo competitions** to show off their ranching skills, including cattle roping. A lasso is used by the rider to catch the steer.

ALASKA

CHUKCHI SEA

Wainwright
Point Hope
Barrow

St. Lawrence
Island

Noatak
Colville

St. Matthew
Island

Nome
Kobuk

BERING SEA
Koyukuk

St. Paul
Island
Hooper Bay
Alakanuk
Yukon
Fort Yukon

Nunivak
Island
Bethel
Kwethluk
Tanana

NEAR
ISLANDS
St. George
Island
Fairbanks

Mount McKinley
6194 m

RAT
ISLANDS
Dillingham

ALEUTIAN ISLANDS
Anchorage

ANDREANOF
ISLANDS
FOX
ISLANDS
Unimak
Island
Kenai
Seward
Cordova

Kodiak

Kodiak
Island
Yakutat

Gulf of
Alaska

PACIFIC
OCEAN
Juneau

Sitka

Ketchikan

CANADA

Facts and Stats

• Montana is 380,847 km² in area – 3.5 times the area of Iceland.

• Seattle [D4] is the biggest city with 3.5 million people. This would fill 35 Olympic stadiums.

• Alaska's Mount McKinley [B11] is the highest mountain at 6194 m – 19 times higher than the Eiffel Tower.

Did You Know?

In 1867, the USA bought Alaska from Russia for $7.2 million (£3.7 million) – cheaper than a modern New York apartment.

Williston
Minot

Great Falls
Fort Peck
Lake
Missouri

Lake
Sakakawea
Grand Forks

MONTANA
NORTH DAKOTA

GREAT PLAINS

Miles City
Bismarck
Jamestown
Fargo

MINNESOTA

Bozeman
Billings

Lake
Oahe
Aberdeen

Watertown

Yellowstone
National Park
Cody
Cheyenne
Pierre

BIGHORN
MOUNTAINS
Gillette
SOUTH DAKOTA

Jackson
Rapid City
White

Sioux Falls

Mount
Rushmore
Lake
Francis
Case

WYOMING
Casper
Yanktown

Niobrara

SAND HILLS
Norfolk

Rock Springs
Loup
IOWA

Laramie
NEBRASKA

Cheyenne
North Platte
Grand Island
Omaha

COLORADO
Platte
Lincoln

Hastings

THE DISTANCE of the USA's Pacific coastline is 12,268 km and would take a migrating whale about 50 days to swim.

KANSAS

25

Southwest USA and Hawaii

The nation's most dramatic landscape belongs to southwest USA, which is covered by the Rocky Mountains. Southern California, Nevada and Arizona are desert – the driest place being Death Valley. Texas is the home of the oil industry, and Nevada's Las Vegas attracts tourists visiting casinos and nearby scenery, such as the Grand Canyon. California has boomed due to the Hollywood film studios, Silicon Valley's large number of computer firms, and some of the most productive farmland in the country. Tropical Hawaii is a popular surfing and beach island 4800 km southwest of California.

Search and Find

Arizona
■ Phoenix F7
California
■ Sacramento . . . C4
Colorado
■ Denver C10
Hawaii
■ Honolulu H3
Kansas
■ Topeka D13

Nevada
■ Carson City . . . C5
New Mexico
■ Santa Fe F10
Oklahoma
■ Oklahoma City. F13
Texas
■ Austin H13
Utah
■ Salt Lake City . . C8

Did You Know?

If California were its own country, it would have the eighth largest economy in the world.

Facts and Stats

- Texas is 691,027 km² in area – 6.5 times the area of Iceland.
- Los Angeles [F5] is the biggest city with 12.9 million people. This would fill 129 Olympic stadiums.
- Mount Whitney [D5] is the highest mountain at 4418 m in height – 14 times higher than the Eiffel Tower.

Map labels

OREGON
IDAHO
Mount Shasta 4322 m
Eureka
PACIFIC OCEAN
Redding
Winnemucca
Humboldt
Elko
Great Salt L.
COAST RANGES
SIERRA NEVADA
Reno
Carson City
NEVADA
Santa Rosa
Sacramento
Oakland
Stockton
San Francisco
Yosemite National Park
Palo Alto
Modesto
Sunnyvale
San Jose
Tonopah
GREAT BASIN
Salinas
Fresno
Monterey
Cedar City
Mount Whitney 4418 m
DEATH VALLEY
San Luis Obispo
Bakersfield
Las Vegas
CALIFORNIA
Hoover Dam
Grand Canyon
Santa Barbara
ARIZONA
Oxnard
Pasadena
San Bernardino
Los Angeles
Riverside
Long Beach
Anaheim
Prescott
Oceanside
Phoenix
San Diego
Gila
Me
Yuma

Mount Kawaikini 1598 m
Kauai
Kapaa
KAUAI CHANNEL
Oahu
Niihau
Waialua
Kaneohe
Wahiawa
Honolulu
Kalaupapa
Maui
Molokai
Lanai City
Wailuku
Lanai
Kahoolawe
ALENUIHAHA CHANNEL
PACIFIC OCEAN
Mauna Kea 4205 m
Hilo
HAWAII
Mauna Loa 4169 m

0 50 100 150 mi
0 100 200 km

The Colorado river has carved a gorge over millions of years to form the **Grand Canyon** [E7]. It is up to 446 km in length and 1.6 km in depth.

0 50 100 150 200 mi

0 100 200 300 km

WYOMING

Brigham City
Ogden

Salt Lake City

Provo

UTAH

Grand Junction

Colorado

Durango
Farmington

mphreys Peak
3851 m

lagstaff
Winslow

ucson

Douglas

Deming

MEXICO

ROCKY MOUNTAINS

Fort Collins
Greeley
Boulder
Lakewood
Denver
Aspen

Mount Elbert
4399 m

Pueblo

Arkansas

Gallup
Los Alamos
Santa Fe
Albuquerque

NEW MEXICO

Rio Grande

Silver City

Las Cruces
El Paso

Sterling

South Platte

COLORADO

Colorado
Springs

Lamar

Roswell

Hobbs
Carlsbad

Pecos

Pecos

NEBRASKA

St. Joseph

Hays
Salina
Kansas
Topeka
Kansas City

KANSAS

Dodge City
Hutchinson
Wichita

Cimarron

Ponca City
Enid

North Canadian

Tulsa
Muskogee

OKLAHOMA

Oklahoma City

Amarillo
Elk City
Norman

MISSOURI

ARKANSAS

Clovis

Lubbock
Wichita Falls
Durant

Plano
Garland
Fort Worth
Dallas
Arlington
Longview
Tyler

Sabine

LOUISIANA

Abilene

Odessa
Midland

San Angelo

TEXAS

Brazos
Leon
Waco
Trinity

STOCKTON PLATEAU

EDWARDS PLATEAU

Colorado

Austin

Beaumont
Houston
Pasadena
Port Arthur
Galveston

Del Rio
San Antonio

San Antonio

Eagle Pass

Laredo

MEXICO

Corpus Christi

GULF OF MEXICO

Brownsville

In the next ...the Hoover Dam's [E6] power station will generate enough electricity to power 34.6 million light bulbs. **minute...**

THE DISTANCE across the Rocky Mountains [E9] is 1700 km and once took horse-drawn wagon trains more than six months to travel.

Lawton

Canada

Canada is the second largest country in the world. The Rocky Mountains of western Canada reach more than 3600 m above sea level and create stunning scenery. Tourists sail along the coast to see icebergs and to view migrating whales. The largest Canadian cities are Toronto and Montreal in the east, and Vancouver in the west. Quebec differs from the rest of Canada because of the large French-speaking population that lives there. Canada has a wealth of natural resources, including wood and petroleum, and is one of the top ten richest nations.

| 0 | 100 | 200 | 300 | 400 | 500 mi |
| 0 | 200 | 400 | 600 | 800 km |

Did You Know?

Canada has 10 percent of the world's forests. These are inhabited by a wide range of wildlife, including bears and moose.

Facts and Stats

• Canada is the second largest country in the world with an area of 9,970,610 km² – 97 times the area of Iceland.

• Toronto [J11] is the biggest city with a population of 5.6 million – this would fill 56 Olympic stadiums.

Deep in the Canadian Rockies is **Banff National Park** in Alberta, which was founded in 1885, and is Canada's oldest national park. Peyto Lake is a popular attraction as the water turns turquoise in colour as the surrounding glaciers melt.

ARCTIC OCEAN

BEAUFORT SEA

Bank Islan

ALASKA (US)

• Inuvik

Mackenzie

• Kugluktuk

• Dawson

Norman Wells •

Mount Logan 5959 m

YUKON TERRITORY

NORTHWEST TERRITORIES

MACKENZIE MOUNTAINS

Gulf of Alaska

■ Whitehorse

Yellowknife ■

Fort Resolution •

ROCKY

Fort Smith •

PACIFIC OCEAN

BRITISH COLUMBIA

C A N

Peace

• Hazelton

• Prince Rupert

COAST

• Peace River

QUEEN CHARLOTTE ISLANDS

MOUNTAINS

• Grande Prairie

ALBERTA

Prince George

MOUNTAINS

■ Edmon

Vancouver Island

Fraser

• Red De

Vancouver •

• Kamloops

• Calgary

Victoria ■

Medicine Hat •

Lethbridge •

UNITED STAT

▷ **Aurora Borealis** *can be seen in the Northern Hemisphere. Also known as the Northern Lights, the bands of shimmering light are caused by atmospheric particles crashing into the Earth's atmosphere.*

Search and Find

Alberta
■ Edmonton H7
British Columbia
■ Victoria I5
Canada
● Ottawa I12
Manitoba
■ Winnipeg I9
New Brunswick
■ Fredericton . . I13
Newfoundland and Labrador
■ St. John's . . . H14
Northwest Territories
■ Yellowknife F7

Nova Scotia
■ Halifax I13
Nunavut
■ Iqaluit F11
Ontario
■ Toronto J11
Prince Edward Island
■ Charlottetown . I13
Quebec
■ Quebec I12
Saskatchewan
■ Regina I8
Yukon Territory
■ Whitehorse . . . F5

GREENLAND
(DENMARK)

Axel Heiberg Island
Ellesmere Island
Bathurst Island
Devon Island
Baffin Bay
Prince of Wales Island
Baffin Island
Victoria Island

● Iqalukyuuttiaq

NUNAVUT

Southampton Island
● Salliit
Iqaluit ■

LABRADOR SEA

Kangiqtiniq ●
(Rankin Inlet)

Coats Island
Mansel Island
Ungava Peninsula

Hudson Strait

Feuilles

● Nain

LABRADOR

In the next ...Canadians will consume 25 litres of maple syrup – a natural sugar from the sugar maple tree. **minute...**

HUDSON BAY

Churchill ●

Churchill
Nelson

NEWFOUNDLAND AND LABRADOR

Goose Bay ●

La Grande Rivière

● Gander
St. John's ■
Newfoundland

C A N A D A

James Bay

Flin Flon ●
Prince Albert
MANITOBA
Severn

● Fort Albany
Albany

ONTARIO

QUEBEC

Anticosti Island

Gaspé ●

PRINCE EDWARD ISLAND

ST. PIERRE AND MIQUELON (FRANCE)

Saskatoon ●

Chicoutimi ●

■ Charlottetown

NEW BRUNSWICK

Regina ●
oose
aw
Brandon ●
■ Winnipeg

Fredericton ■
Quebec ●
St. John
■ Halifax

Bay of Fundy
NOVA SCOTIA

● Thunder Bay

Trois-Rivières ●
Sherbrooke ●

AMERICA

Sudbury ●
Montreal ●

Ottawa ●

Georgian Bay

ATLANTIC OCEAN

Toronto ■ ● Oshawa
Kitchener ● ● Hamilton
● London

THE DISTANCE from St. John's [H14] to Vancouver [I6] is further than St. John's to Prague, Europe.

● Windsor

Mexico

1 2 3 4 5 6 7

Did You Know?

Modern chewing gum is made from the same gum the Aztecs chewed, with added sweetener to make it more tasty.

Tijuana

Mexicali

Ensenada

UNITED STATES OF AMERICA

Ciudad Juárez

Rio Grande

Mexico lies between the USA and Guatemala, and has two high coastal mountain ranges, between which is a high plateau called the Altiplano. Much of the land is mountain or desert, making rural areas very poor as less than one-fifth is suitable for farming. As a result, many people move to Mexico City or the USA for work – more than 20 million people now live in the Mexico City area. Tourists visit both the tropical beaches and the ancient sites of the Aztec and Mayan cultures.

Guadalupe Island

Cedros Island

Hermosillo

Chihuahua

Gulf of California

Guaymas

Ciudad Obregón

Los Mochis

Culiacán

La Paz

Durango

Mazatlán

In the next

...Mexico's farmers will use 10 million litres of water on the land – enough for 2.5 million baths.

minute...

World Record

At 430 m above the ground, the Baluarte Bridge in northern Mexico is the world's highest suspension bridge.

MARÍAS ISLANDS

Tep

TEOTIHUACÁN [H9] was Mexico's biggest Aztec city. Ruins include the Pyramid of the Sun in the Avenue of the Dead.

Socorro Island

PACIFIC OCEAN

The Mayan civilization lasted 2000 years and many magnificent buildings were constructed. **Palenque** *[H12] is a site of ancient Mayan ruins, including the Palenque Palace.*

The stories of the ancient Mexican cultures are retold through ornately dressed **folk dancers**. The costumes and performances represent ancient Mayan dances for the gods.

Facts and Stats

• Mexico City [H9] has a population of 20.1 million people – this would fill 201 Olympic stadiums.

• The Rio Grande [C7] is 3060 km in length – less than half the length of the Nile river.

• The highest mountain is Volcan Pico de Orizaba [H10] at 5700 m in height. It is 18 times higher than the Eiffel Tower.

THE DISTANCE from east to west across Mexico City [H9] is only 30 km, but it takes more than three hours by car at peak times.

The Xochimilco area of Mexico City [H9] has many **ancient canals**. During festivals, boats are covered with flowers to attract tourists.

UNITED STATES OF AMERICA

Nuevo Laredo

ómez Palacio • Monclova

Terreón • Monterrey • Reynosa • Matamoros

Saltillo •

MEXICO

GULF OF MEXICO

• Ciudad Victoria

Ciudad Madero

San Luis Potosí • Tampico

• Aguascalientes

Cancún •

Mérida • *Cozumel Island*

León • *Chichén Itzá*

Querétaro • *Yucatán Peninsula*

• Guadalajara

Bay of Campeche

Pachuca

Teotihuacán ◆

Morelia • Ecatepec

Colima • Toluca *Volcan Pico de Orizaba 5700 m*

Mexico City Veracruz

Cuernavaca • Puebla • Orizaba

Chetumal

Coatzacoalcos • Villahermosa

Chilpancingo • *Palenque* ◆

Oaxaca •

Tuxtla Gutiérrez •

Acapulco •

GUATEMALA

BELIZE

Gulf of Tehuantepec

0	100	200	300 mi

0	200	400 km

South and Central America

BAHAMAS

CUBA

DOMINICAN
REPUBLIC

BELIZE

GUATEMALA

HONDURAS

EL SALVADOR

NICARAGUA

COSTA RICA

PANAMA

VENEZUELA

GUYANA

SURINAME

COLOMBIA

ECUADOR

PERU

BRAZIL

BOLIVIA

PACIFIC
OCEAN

CHILE

PARAGUAY

URUGUAY

ATLANTIC
OCEAN

ARGENTINA

2

1

3

4

5

6

7

9

8

10

KEY
1 HAITI
2 JAMAICA
3 ST. KITTS AND NEVIS
4 ANTIGUA AND BARBUDA
5 DOMINICA
6 ST. LUCIA
7 ST. VINCENT AND THE GRENADINES
8 GRENADA
9 BARBADOS
10 TRINIDAD AND TOBAGO

COUNTRY FACTFILE

Country	Life expectancy	Population in thousands	Population growth %	Population as urban %	Literacy %	Area km²	Population density per km²	Capital city	Currency	Languages
Antigua and Barbuda	76	86	1.3	59	86	442	194.6	St. John's	East Caribbean Dollar	English, Creole
Argentina	77	40,117	1	92	97	2,766,890	14.5	Buenos Aires	Argentine Peso	Spanish
Bahamas	71	354	0.9	87	96	13,939	25.3	Nassau	Bahamian Dollar	English, Creole
Barbados	75	274	0.4	52	99	430	637.2	Bridgetown	Barbadian Dollar	English, Bajan (Creole)
Belize	68	333	2.1	52	77	22,965	14.5	Belmopan	Belizean Dollar	English, Creole, Spanish
Bolivia	68	10,426	1.7	67	87	1,098,581	9.5	La Paz, Sucre	Boliviano	Spanish, Quechua, Aymara
Brazil	73	185,713	1.1	87	89	8,547,404	21.7	Brasília	Real	Portuguese
Chile	78	17,094	0.8	89	96	756,626	22.6	Santiago, Valparaiso	Chilean Peso	Spanish
Colombia	75	46,045	1.2	75	90	1,414,568	40.3	Bogotá	Colombian Peso	Spanish
Costa Rica	78	4302	1.3	65	95	51,100	84.2	San José	Costa Rican Colon	Spanish
Cuba	78	11,241	0.0	74	99	110,861	101.4	Havana	Cuban Peso	Spanish
Dominica	76	71	0.0	71	94	739	96.1	Roseau	East Caribbean Dollar	English, French Creole
Dominican Republic	77	9379	1.3	69	87	48,443	193.6	Santo Domingo	Dominican Peso	Spanish
Ecuador	76	14,483	1.4	67	91	269,178	53.8	Quito	US Dollar	Spanish, Quechua
El Salvador	74	6183	0.3	64	81	21,041	293.9	San Salvador	US Dollar	Spanish
Grenada	73	103	0.6	39	96	344	299.4	St. George's	East Caribbean Dollar	English, French Creole
Guatemala	71	14,362	2	49	69.1	108,889	131.9	Guatemala City	Quetzal	Spanish
Guyana	67	754	0.0	36	92	215,083	3.5	Georgetown	Guyanese Dollar	English, Creole
Haiti	63	9923	0.8	52	53	27,750	357.6	Port-au-Prince	Gourde	French, Creole
Honduras	71	8046	1.9	52	80	112,088	71.8	Tegucigalpa	Lempira	Spanish
Jamaica	73	2706	0.7	53	88	10,991	246.2	Kingston	Jamaican Dollar	English, Creole
Nicaragua	72	5742	1.1	57	68	130,670	43.9	Managua	Gold Cordoba	Spanish
Panama	78	3406	1.4	75	92	75,990	44.8	Panama City	Balboa, US Dollar	Spanish, English
Paraguay	76	6230	1.3	61	94	406,752	15.3	Asunción	Guarani	Spanish, Guarani
Peru	73	30,136	1	77	93	1,285,216	23.4	Lima	Nuevo Sol	Spanish, Quechua
St. Kitts and Nevis	75	52	0.8	43	97	269	193.3	Basseterre	East Caribbean Dollar	English, Creole
St. Lucia	77	166	0.4	48	90	617	269	Castries	East Caribbean Dollar	English, French Creole
St. Vincent and the Grenadines	74	109	0.0	55	96	398	280.2	Kingstown	East Caribbean Dollar	English, Creole
Suriname	71	525	1.1	75	90	163,270	3.2	Paramaribo	Suriname Dollar	Dutch, Sranantonga, Hindi
Trinidad and Tobago	72	1318	0.0	72	99	5128	257	Port-of-Spain	Trinidad and Tobago Dollar	English, Creole
Uruguay	76	3252	0.2	92	98	176,215	18.5	Montevideo	Uruguayan Peso	Spanish
Venezuela	74	27,150	1.5	93	93	912,050	29.8	Caracas	Bolivar	Spanish

Central America and the Caribbean

Central America is a narrow area of land where the mountain chain continues from Antarctica up to Alaska. The only gap, which joins the Atlantic and Pacific Oceans, is the Panama Canal. The manmade canal shortens the journey between the oceans by 13,000 km. The Caribbean islands are mainly agricultural, but their sandy beaches, warm seas and links to the USA and Europe make them popular tourist destinations. Venezuela is one of the world's leading oil producers and is much wealthier than Colombia and Guyana.

In many places in Central America, **weaving** is still done by hand rather than by machine. Colourful rugs and tapestries from the region are sold around the world.

MEXICO

Guanabacoa
Havana • Cárdenas
Pinar del Río • Santa Clara
Nueva Gerona • Cienfuegos • CUI
Isla de la Juventud Sancti Spíritu
Camagüey

CAYMAN ISLANDS (UK)

Montego Bay
JAMAICA
Spar
Tov

BELIZE
• Belize City
MAYA MOUNTAINS • Belmopan
Quezaltenango
• San Antonio
GUATEMALA
San Pedro • La Ceiba
Guatemala Sula • El Progreso
City
Escuintla • HONDURAS
• Tegucigalpa
San Salvador •
EL SALVADOR
• Estelí
Chinandega • NICARAGUA
León • Managua

COSTA RICA
San José Gulf of Barranq
Puntarenas • • Limón Darien
Cerro Chirripó Panama Colón Cartagena
Grande 3819 m Canal • San Miguelito
CORDILLERA CENTRAL Sincelejo
David • Panama City Monter
PANAMA
Gulf of
Panama

Medellín
Quibdó •
Manizales
Pereira •
Armenia •
Buenaventura • Ibagué
Cali •
Popayán •
Pasto • CORDILLERA

ECUADOR

Search and Find

0   100   200   300   400 mi
0   200   400   600 km

Facts and Stats

• Colombia has a population of 46 million people – this would fill 460 Olympic stadiums.

• The life expectancy of people in Haiti is only 63 years, compared to 78 years in Cuba and a world average of 68 years.

• The average income per person in Haiti is £430 and £15,060 in the Bahamas, compared to a world average of £5640.

A

Nassau

There are two lakes
in the craters of the
Poas volcano, Costa Rica.
Due to geothermal activity,
it is believed that the lakes
are turning into geysers.
Since 1828, the volcano
has erupted 39 times.

B

BAHAMAS

TURKS AND
CAICOS ISLANDS
(UK)

Holguín
ayamo
• Guantánamo
iago Cap-Haïtien •
Cuba Gonaïves •
Port-au-Prince •
gston
Les Cayes • Jacmel •

DOMINICAN
REPUBLIC
Santiago San Francisco
de Macorís •
La Vega •
La Romana •
Santo
Domingo

VIRGIN
ISLANDS
(UK)

VIRGIN
ISLANDS | ANGUILLA (UK)
(US)

ST. MARTIN (FRANCE)/SINT MAARTEN (NETH.)

ST. BARTHELÉMY (FRANCE)

ST. EUSTATIUS (NETH.)

C

PUERTO
RICO (US)

SABA
(NETH.)

Basseterre •
ST. KITTS AND NEVIS
MONTSERRAT (UK)

ANTIGUA AND
BARBUDA
St. John's •

D

HAITI

GUADELOUPE
(FRANCE)

CARIBBEAN SEA

DOMINICA
• Roseau

MARTINIQUE (FRANCE)

In the next
...Venezuela
will extract
enough oil from
the Earth to make
220,000 litres
of petrol.
minute...

ST. LUCIA
• Castries

ARUBA
(NETHERLANDS)

CURAÇAO
(NETHERLANDS)

ST. VINCENT AND
THE GRENADINES
• Kingstown

BARBADOS
• Bridgetown

E

BONAIRE
(NETHERLANDS)

GRENADA
• St. George's

World Record

Pico Cristobal Colon
5800 m
• Maracaibo
ta
rta
edad
Barquisimeto •
Valera •
• Acarigua
• Guanare
• Barinas

Port-of-Spain

• Cumaná
• Valencia • Barcelona
Caracas

TRINIDAD
AND TOBAGO

At more than
979 m in height,
Angel Falls [G11] is
the highest waterfall
in the world.

F

úcuta •
• San Cristóbal
• Bucaramanga
rrancabermeja

Ciudad Bolívar •

Ciudad Guayana •

• Georgetown

G

• Tunja

VENEZUELA

Angel Falls ◆

Paramaribo

Río Meta

• Puerto Ayacucho

GUIANA
HIGHLANDS

Bogotá
• Villavicencio

GUYANA

FRENCH
GUIANA
(FRANCE)

SURINAME

H

COLOMBIA

BRAZIL

BRAZIL

Río Vaupés

BRAZIL

Río Apaporis

I

o Caquetá

Did You Know?

PERU

THE DISTANCE from one end
of the Panama Canal [F6] to the
other is only 77 km, but it saves
18 days sailing time.

The Bermuda Triangle is an area
in the Atlantic Ocean, northeast
of the Caribbean. Many ships
and aircraft have disappeared
here without a trace.

J

South America

Stretching from the tropical forests of the Amazon to just a short distance from icy Antarctica, South America is a continent of contrasts. The Andes stretch the length of the continent, but the main feature is the Amazon rainforest. The rainforest is home to more plant and animal species than any other habitat in the world. However, more than 50,000 km² of the rainforest is destroyed each year to make room for farmland. The forest not only provides a home to many animals, but it is also the source of many plant-derived medicines. By absorbing carbon dioxide, the forest helps to reduce global warming.

At 6448 km in length, the **Amazon river** crosses the full width of Brazil. A wide range of wildlife live in the river, including the endangered boto, or Amazon river dolphin.

PACIFIC OCEAN

Search and Find

Argentina
• Buenos Aires . . G8
Bolivia
• La Paz D7
• Sucre E7
Brazil
• Brasília D10
Chile
• Santiago G7

• Valparaíso G6
Ecuador
• Quito B5
Paraguay
• Asunción E8
Peru
• Lima D5
Uruguay
• Montevideo . . . G8

In the next
...9000 tonnes of the Amazon rainforest will be destroyed – about 100 trees and other plants.
minute...

The statue of Jesus, **Christ the Redeemer**, stands at the top of Mount Corcovado, Rio de Janeiro [E10]. At 38 m in height, it is one of the most famous landmarks in the world.

Map labels

VENEZUE
Esmeraldas
Ibarra
Manta • Quito
Portoviejo • Ambato
Guayaquil • Riobamba
ECUADOR
COLOMBIA
Negro
Iquitos
AMAZON BASIN
Amazon
Piura
Chiclayo
Pucallpa
Porto Velho
Trujillo
Chimbote
PERU
Rio Branco
Huacho • Lima
Callao • Huancayo
Ayacucho • Cusco **BOLIVI**
Ica
Lake Titicaca
Juliaca • Puno
Arequipa •
La Paz Oruro Cochabam
Arica Sucre
Nevado Sajama
6520 m
Iquique • Potosí
Tarija
Calama • San Salva de Jujuy
ATACAMA DESERT
Antofagasta •
CHILE
La Serena • Córdo
Coquimbo •
San Juan
Godoy Cruz
Viña del Mar • Mendoza
Valparaíso
Santiago
Rancagua Cerro Aconcagua 6959 m
Talcahuano • Chillán
Concepción •
Los Ángeles
Temuco • Neuqué
Valdivia •
Osorno • Comodo
Puerto Montt Rivadav
PATAGONIA
Puert
Madr
Río Galle
Punta Arenas •
Ushu
ARG

GUYANA
SURINAME
FRENCH GUIANA (FRANCE)

Amapá
Macapá
Marajó Island
Belém
São Luis
Parnaíba
Manaus
Amazon
Santarém
Altamira
Fortaleza
Marabá
Imperatriz
Teresina
Mossoró
Campina Grande
Natal
João Pessoa
Araguaína
Juazeiro do Norte
Recife
BRAZIL
Tocantins
Juazeiro
Maceio
Aracaju
Feira de Santana
Salvador
Chiabá
Taguatinga
Brasília
Itabuna
MATO GROSSO PLATEAU
Anápolis
Goiânia
Campo Grande
Uberlândia
Uberaba
Governador Valadares
Rio Préto
Belo Horizonte
Pedro Juan Caballero
Nova Iguaçu
Vitoria
PARAGUAY
Campinas
São Paulo
Niteroi
Rio de Janeiro
Asunción
Ciudad del Este
Santos
ACO
Resistencia
Curitiba
Corrientes
TINA
Florianópolio
Salto
Rivera
Pelotas
Porto Alegre
nta Fe
Rivera
Rio Grande
osario
URUGUAY
Buenos Aires
Montevideo
omas
Zamora
La Plata
Bahía Blanca
Mar del Plata
Punta Alta

ATLANTIC OCEAN

FALKLAND ISLANDS (UK)

SOUTH GEORGIA (UK)

e Horn

0	200	400	600	800 mi
0	400	800	1200 km	

Facts and Stats

• Brazil's population is 185.7 million and would fill 1857 Olympic stadiums. In comparison, Uruguay's population is only 3.3 million.

• There are only 9 doctors per 10,000 people in Peru, compared to 37 doctors in Uruguay and a world average of 23 doctors.

• The average income per person in Uruguay is £7560 and £810 in Bolivia, compared to a world average of £5640.

Did You Know?

The Amazon river holds two-thirds of all the flowing water in the world and is 270 km in width where it meets the sea.

Extreme Weather

Chile's Atacama Desert [E7] has an average rainfall of less than 0.5 mm a year. The city of Calama [E7] has never recorded a single drop. It's too dry for animals to survive.

USHUAIA [J7] is the most southern city in the world. It has a ski resort and a base for supply ships to Antarctica.

THE DISTANCE from Chile to the next land mass of Australia is 10,400 km and would take 12 hours by plane.

One of the largest **street carnivals** in the world is held every February in Rio de Janeiro [E10]. People dress in elaborate costumes and parades take place in the city centre. More than 200,000 people take part.

Europe

ARCTIC OCEAN

ICELAND

FINLAND

NORWAY   SWEDEN

ESTONIA

LATVIA

DENMARK

1   2

RUSSIAN
FEDERATION

UNITED
KINGDOM

REPUBLIC OF
IRELAND

3

POLAND

BELARUS

GERMANY

4

6

UKRAINE

ATLANTIC
OCEAN

5

11

10

7

9

8

FRANCE

12

15

ROMANIA

16

13   14

23

17   18

BULGARIA

GEORGIA

19   21

AZERBAIJAN

24

20   22

26

SPAIN

ITALY

GREECE

PORTUGAL

25

KEY

1 RUSSIAN FEDERATION	14 MONACO
2 LITHUANIA	15 SLOVENIA
3 NETHERLANDS	16 CROATIA
4 BELGIUM	17 BOSNIA AND HERZEGOVINA
5 LUXEMBOURG	18 SERBIA
6 CZECH REPUBLIC	19 MONTENEGRO
7 SLOVAKIA	20 KOSOVO
8 MOLDOVA	21 MACEDONIA
9 HUNGARY	22 ALBANIA
10 AUSTRIA	23 SAN MARINO
11 LIECHTENSTEIN	24 VATICAN CITY
12 SWITZERLAND	25 MALTA
13 ANDORRA	26 ARMENIA

COUNTRY FACTFILE

Country	Life expectancy	Population in thousands	Population growth %	Population as urban %	Literacy %	Area km²	Population density per km²	Capital city	Currency	Languages
Albania	78	2832	−0.3	52	99	28,748	98.5	Tiranë	Lek	Albanian
Andorra	83	78	0.3	95	100	468	166.7	Andorra la Vella	Euro	Catalan, Spanish
Armenia	73	3262	0.0	70	99	29,743	109.7	Yerevan	Dram	Armenian
Austria	80	8404	0.03	68	98	83,858	100.2	Vienna	Euro	German
Azerbaijan*	71	9111	0.8	57	99	86,600	105.2	Baku	Manat	Azeri
Belarus	71	9481	−0.4	75	99	207,546	45.7	Minsk	Belarusian Rouble	Belarusian, Russian
Belgium	80	10,951	0.07	97	99	30,528	358.7	Brussels	Euro	Dutch, French
Bosnia and Herzegovina	79	3840	0.0	49	97	51,129	75.1	Sarajevo	Marka	Croat, Serb
Bulgaria	74	7365	−0.8	71	98	110,993	66.4	Sofia	Lev	Bulgarian, Turkish
Croatia	76	4291	−0.05	58	98	56,542	75.9	Zagreb	Kuna	Croat
Czech Republic	77	10,562	0.0	75	99	78,864	133.9	Prague	Czech Koruna	Czech
Denmark	79	5581	0.3	87	100	43,094	129.5	Copenhagen	Danish Krone	Danish
Estonia	74	1318	−0.6	69	100	45,227	29.1	Tallinn	Euro	Estonian, Russian
Finland	79	5401	0.1	85	100	338,145	15.9	Helsinki	Euro	Finnish, Swedish
France	81	62,466	0.5	85	99	547,030	114.2	Paris	Euro	French
Georgia	77	4472	−0.3	68	99	69,492	68.6	Tbilisi	Lari	Georgian
Germany	80	81,752	−0.2	88	99	357,021	229	Berlin	Euro	German
Greece	80	10,788	−0.9	61	96	131,957	81.8	Athens	Euro	Greek
Hungary	75	9982	−0.2	68	99	93,030	107.3	Budapest	Forint	Hungarian
Iceland	81	320	0.7	93	100	102,819	3.1	Reykjavik	Icelandic Krona	Icelandic
Ireland, Republic of	78	4240	1.1	61	99	70,285	60.3	Dublin	Euro	English, Irish (Gaelic)
Italy	82	60,340	0.4	68	99	301,277	200.3	Rome	Euro	Italian
Kosovo	78	1734	−0.5	51	92	10,910	158.9	Pristina	Euro	Albania
Latvia	73	2068	−0.6	69	100	64,610	32	Riga	Latvian Lat	Latvian, Russian
Liechtenstein	82	36.1	0.7	45	100	160	225.6	Vaduz	Swiss Franc	German
Lithuania	76	3054	−0.3	68	100	65,301	46.8	Vilnius	Litas	Lithuanian, Russian
Luxembourg	80	512	1.1	88	100	2586	198	Luxembourg	Euro	Letzeburgish, German, French
Macedonia	75	2057	0.2	67	96	25,713	80	Skopje	Macedonian Denar	Macedonian, Albanian
Malta	80	418	0.4	95	93	316	1327	Valletta	Euro	Maltese, English
Moldova	70	4090	0.0	48	99	33,873	120.7	Chisinau	Moldovan Leu	Romanian (Moldovan), Russian, Ukrainian
Monaco	90	31.1	0.0	100	99	2	15,550	Monaco	Euro	French, Monegasque, Italian
Montenegro	75	620	−0.01	61	97	13,812	45.8	Podgorica	Euro	Serb, Albanian, Montenegrin
Netherlands	81	16,575	0.4	91	99	41,526	399.1	Amsterdam, The Hague	Euro	Dutch, Frisian
Norway	80	4986	0.3	79	100	323,878	15.4	Oslo	Norwegian Krone	Norwegian
Poland	76	38,325	0.02	66	100	312,685	122.6	Warsaw	Zloty	Polish
Portugal	79	10,562	0.0	64	93	92,391	114.3	Lisbon	Euro	Portuguese
Romania	74	19,043	−0.4	57	97	237,500	80.2	Bucharest	Leu	Romanian, Hungarian
Russian Federation	66	142,905	−0.5	78	99	17,075,400	8.4	Moscow	Rouble	Russian, Tatar, Ukrainian
San Marino	83	32.2	1.0	94	98	61	527.9	San Marino	Euro	Italian
Serbia	75	7121	−0.5	56	96	77,468	91.9	Belgrade	Serbian Dinar	Serb, Hungarian
Slovakia	76	5397	0.0	57	100	49,036	110.1	Bratislava	Euro	Slovak, Hungarian
Slovenia	77	2047	0.0	51	100	20,273	101	Ljubljana	Euro	Slovenian
Spain	81	47,190	0.06	78	98	504,782	93.5	Madrid	Euro	Spanish (Castilian), Catalan, Basque, Gallego
Sweden	81	9483	0.2	85	99	449,964	21.1	Stockholm	Swedish Krona	Swedish
Switzerland	81	7786	0.2	74	99	41,285	188.6	Bern	Swiss Franc	German, French, Italian
Ukraine	69	45,779	−0.6	69	99	603,700	75.8	Kiev	Hryvnia	Ukrainian, Russian
United Kingdom	80	62,262	0.6	82	99	244,088	255.1	London	British Pound	English
Vatican City	N/A	0.44	N/A	100	100	0.44	1009.1	Vatican City	Euro	Italian, Latin

* Although Azerbaijan is a member of some European organizations, it is historically and culturally part of western Asia
NB: Cyprus is part of Europe, but the mapping can be found in the Asia section

The British Isles

The United Kingdom (England, Scotland, Wales and Northern Ireland) and the Republic of Ireland make up the British Isles. The UK has become one of the most influential and prosperous countries in the world. By 1900, the British Empire ruled many countries, including Canada, South Africa, India and Australia, which is why so many nations speak English. Ireland declared independence in 1919, but it only came into effect in 1922. Scotland, Wales and Northern Ireland now have their own parliaments. Manufacturing was once the major industry, but most wealth is now generated by banking, insurance and high-tech equipment.

The **Giant's Causeway** [E7] in Northern Ireland is made up of 40,000 columns created by a volcanic eruption. The columns measure up to 12 m in height. According to legend, the giant Finn McCool began to build the causeway towards Scotland, but he fell asleep before he finished it.

Search and Find

England		Scotland	
• London	H10	■ Edinburgh	E8
Northern Ireland		**Wales**	
■ Belfast	F7	■ Cardiff	H8
Republic of Ireland			
• Dublin	G7		

THE DISTANCE from Land's End [I7] to John o'Groats [C9] once took a cyclist 41 hours and a runner 12 days to complete.

ATLANTIC OCEAN

OUTER HEBRIDES

Lewis

Skye

Giant's Causeway

• Londonderr

NORTHERN IRELAND ■

Sligo •

Bel

REPUBLIC OF IRELAND

• Arma

Drogheda •

IRIS SEA

Galway •

Liffey ● **Dubl**

Shannon

WICKLOW MOUNTAINS

Limerick •

ST. GEORGE'S CHANNEL

Carrantuohill 1041 m

Waterford •

Cork •

Edinburgh [E8], Scotland, is the second most visited city after London. More than 13 million people are attracted to the city each year to see historical sights, such as Edinburgh Castle, or to attend the Edinburgh Festival in August.

ISLES OF SCILLY *Land's End*

8 9 10 11 12 13 14

A B C D E F G H I J

SHETLAND ISLANDS

Lerwick

ORKNEY ISLANDS

John o'Groats

Inverness

SCOTLAND

Ben Nevis 1343 m

GRAMPIAN MOUNTAINS

Aberdeen

Perth • Dundee

Falkirk

Glasgow • Edinburgh

Ayr

Newcastle upon Tyne

Carlisle

Scafell Pike 977 m

PENNINES

Sunderland

Middlesbrough

ISLE OF MAN (UK)

York

Blackpool

Leeds

Hull

Snowdon 1085 m

Liverpool Manchester

Chester Sheffield

ENGLAND

Stoke-on-Trent

Trent

Wrexham

Nottingham

WALES

Derby

Aberystwyth

Leicester

Birmingham

Peterborough

Norwich

Coventry

Northampton

Cambridge

Ipswich

Colchester

CAMBRIAN MOUNTAINS

Wye

Severn

Ouse

Swansea

Newport

Gloucester

Swindon

Oxford

Thames

London

Cardiff

Bristol

Avebury Stone Circle

Reading

Stonehenge

Dover

Southampton

Portsmouth

Exeter

Bournemouth

Brighton

Plymouth

Isle of Wight

ENGLISH CHANNEL

Guernsey

CHANNEL Jersey

ISLANDS (UK)

NORTH SEA

Snowdonia National Park [G8], Wales, was created in 1951 and covers 2142 km² of land. More than 26,000 people actually live within the area and it receives more than six million visitors a year. The area is a mixture of forest, open land, coast and mountains – making it popular with hikers.

0 50 100 150 mi
0 100 200 km

THE TOWER OF LONDON [H10] has been a castle, a royal palace, a prison, a zoo and the home of the crown jewels.

In the next ...133 passengers will arrive or depart from London's Heathrow Airport, one of the busiest airports in the world. minute...

Facts and Stats

• London [H10] is the biggest city with 8.3 million people. This would fill 83 Olympic stadiums.

• The Shannon [G6] is the longest river at 386 km in length. However, it is more than 17 times shorter than the Nile river.

• Ben Nevis [D8] is the highest mountain at 1343 m in height – four times higher than the Eiffel Tower.

Did You Know?

Avebury Stone Circle [I9] is 6000 years old, and is the largest ancient stone monument in the world.

*The **Millennium Bridge**, London [H10], was opened in 2000, and is used as a pedestrian footbridge. It has been designed to hold 5000 people at any one time. St. Paul's Cathedral is situated at its north end and the Tate Modern art gallery is at the south end.*

Scandinavia

Norway, Sweden, Denmark, Finland and Iceland are Europe's most northerly and least populated countries. Mainland Scandinavia stretches from Norway's mountainous Atlantic coast in the west to Finland's low-lying forested countryside in the east. More than one-third lies within the Arctic Circle where, during a 73-day winter period, the Sun never rises. Norway and Iceland are not members of the European Union. Living standards are high due to vast natural resources, such as oil, gas, timber and iron. Scandinavia has a reputation for stylish designs with brands such as Bang and Olufsen, Ikea and Volvo.

In the next ...minute...

...Sweden will make more than two million matches – enough to fill 40,000 boxes.

World Record

Finland has more of its territory covered by lakes than any other country – 187,888 lakes cover 10 percent of the country.

Facts and Stats

- Sweden's population of 9.2 million would fill 92 Olympic stadiums.
- The life expectancy of people in Sweden is 81 years, compared to 78 years in Denmark and a world average of 68 years.
- The average income per person in Norway is £19,900, compared to a world average of £3500.

Did You Know?

The first Legoland was opened in Billund [I6], Denmark, in 1968. On average, every person in the world owns 52 Lego bricks.

◁ *Sognefjord [F5], Norway, is the second largest fjord in the world. Towns are situated on the fjord and the stunning scenery attracts many tourists, which helps to support the economy.*

Lofoten Island

Bodø

ATLANTIC OCEAN

Kristiansund • Trondheim • Östersund

Ålesund •

NORWAY

Sognefjord *Galdhøpiggen* 2469 m

Bergen • • Voss • Lillehammer

Hamar •

Haugesund • • Oslo

Drammen •

Stavanger • Skien • Fredrikstad Karlstad

Öreb

Kristiansand • Linköpin

Skagerrak Göteborg Borås

NORTH SEA Jönköpin

Ålborg • *Kattegat*

DENMARK Halmstad Väx

Randers

Århus • Helsingborg Karlshamr

Billund Karlskro

Esbjerg • **Copenhagen** • Lund

Kolding Odense Malmö

Roskilde

BORNHOLM (DENMARK

GERMANY

ARCTIC OCEAN

North Cape

Vadsø

Tromsø

Narvik

Kiruna

LAPLAND

Gällivare

SWEDEN

Rovaniemi

Kemi

Luleå
Piteå

Oulu

Skellefteå

GULF OF BOTHNIA

Umeå

Kokkola

Örnsköldsvik

Kuopio

Vaasa

undsvall

Jyväskylä

FINLAND

Söderhamn

Pori

Tampere

Hämeenlinna

Lahti

Gävle

Åland Island

Turku

Vantaa

Kotka

Espoo

Helsinki

Mariehamn

Uppsala

Västerås

Stockholm

Södertälje

Norrköping

Västervik

BALTIC SEA

Visby

Gotland

Borgholm

RUSSIAN FEDERATION

Sweden's *Ice Hotel* near Kiruna [C8] is only open from December to April and is rebuilt each year. The hotel has more than 80 rooms and even has a church. Everything in the hotel, down to the glasses, is made of ice.

Search and Find

Denmark
• Copenhagen I7
Finland
• Helsinki G10
Iceland
• Reykjavik I11

Norway
• Oslo G6
Sweden
• Stockholm G8

THE DISTANCE from Norway's North Cape [A9] to the North Pole is shorter than the distance from Oslo [G6] to southern Italy.

LAPLAND [C9] is said to be where Santa Claus lives. In December, many tourists visit the region to see Santa with his elves and reindeer.

0   50   100   150 mi
0   100   200 km

Isafjördhur

Olafsfjördhur

Húsavik

Akureyri

Myvatn

Seydisfjördhur

Eskifjördhur

Ólafsvik

ICELAND

VATNAJÖKULL

Hvítá   Thórsá

Akranes

Hvannadalshnúkur 2119 m

Höfn

Reykjavik

Keflavik

Kopavogur

NORWEGIAN SEA

ATLANTIC OCEAN

Vestmannaeyar

Spain and Portugal

The Iberian Peninsula is occupied by Spain and Portugal. Africa is less than 16 km from the Strait of Gibraltar, and to the north Spain is bordered by France and the mountain state of Andorra. Spain also includes the Balearic Islands in the Mediterranean Sea and the Canary Islands, including Tenerife and Gran Canaria, which lie 100 km west of Africa in the Atlantic Ocean. Well-known for olive, orange and lemon groves, as well as hot weather and sandy beaches, these countries attract millions of tourists each year.

◁ The costas of Spain are popular coastal regions. **Costa Brava [C13]** in northeast Spain is in the vicinity of Barcelona. S'Agaró is an exclusive resort, and its hotels have even been used in films.

THE DISTANCE from the east to the west side of the border between Spain and Gibraltar [I7] is only 800 m.

BILBAO [B9] is home to many museums including the Fine Arts Museum and the world-famous Guggenheim Museum.

Facts and Stats

• Spain's population of 47.2 million would fill 472 Olympic stadiums. However, the population of Andorra is only 67,000 and would only fill half a stadium.

• The life expectancy of people in Spain is 81 years, compared to a world average of 68 years.

• The average income per person in Andorra is £27,890, compared to a world average of £5640.

Did You Know?

Sardines are the most popular Portuguese seafood. The average consumption for a person is 6 kg a year.

El Ferrol
La Coruña
Gijón
Ovied
Lugo
CANTABRIAN M
Santiago de Compostela
Sil
León
Orense
Esla
Vigo
Braga
Zamora
Guimaraes
Duero
Tormes
Porto
Salamanca
Aveiro
SIERR
Coimbra
Tajo (Tag
Tajo (Tagus)
Cáceres
Santarém
PORTUGAL
Mérida
Estoril
Lisbon
Badajoz
Almada
Setúbal
Évora
Beja
Guadiana
Guadalqui
ATLANTIC OCEAN
Lagos
Seville
Huelva
Faro
Moron de la Frontera
Arcos
Rond
Jerez de la Frontera
Cádiz
GIBRALT (UK)
Algeciras
Strait of Gibralt
CEUT (SPAI
MOROCC

BAY OF BISCAY

Santander
Bilbao
San Sebastián
FRANCE
NTAINS
Vitória-Gasteiz
Pamplona
Pico de Aneto
3405 m
PYRENEES
ANDORRA
Andorra
la Vella
Logroño
Burgos
Girona
Manresa
Mataró
Palencia
Soria
Gállego
Zaragoza
Lleida
Terrasa
Barcelona
Ebro
Cinca
Costa Brava
Valladolid
Duero
Reus
Tarragona
Costa Dorada
egovia
Tortosa
vila
Guadalajara
Morella
Menorca
Alcalá de Henares
Teruel
Mallorca
Mahón
Madrid
Cuenca
Castellón de la Plana
Costa del Azahar
Palma
Aranjuez
Turia
Toledo
Sagunto
SPAIN
Valencia
Gulf of
Valencia
Ibiza
BALEARIC ISLANDS
Júcar
Albacete
Ibiza
Ciudad Real
Formentera
Alcoy
Benidorm
Segura
Alicante
Elche
Costa Blanca
Linares
Murcia
Córdoba
Jaén
Lorca
Cartagena
Genil
Granada
SIERRA NEVADA
Motril
Almería
Málaga
Marbella
Costa del Sol

MEDITERRANEAN SEA

MELILLA
(SPAIN)

In the next ...the bark of Portugal's and Spain's cork trees will produce enough cork for 136,000 wine bottles. *minute...*

◁ Bullfighting is popular in Spain. **Toreros** are performers who fight and kill bulls. There are various types, including matadors, depending on the skills used during the fight. Performances and costumes are elaborate, attracting tourists from all over the world.

France and Monaco

The third largest country in Europe, France has the fourth highest population. Despite having a rural landscape, more than 85 percent of the population lives in towns, with more than one-sixth in Paris. France has an excellent health, education and social care system, and is the fifth wealthiest country in the world. Northern France is an industrialized, low-lying region, and the south has the snow-capped peaks of the Alps and Pyrenees as well as the sunny beaches of the Mediterranean Sea. Monaco is a tiny, independent, French-speaking country. One of the richest countries in the world, Monaco boasts more than 2000 millionaires and no taxes. Only three hours from the mainland by boat is the mountainous island of Corsica.

Search and Find

France	Monaco
• Paris C9	• Monaco H11

PARIS [C9] is one of the most visited places in the world, with attractions such as the Eiffel Tower and the Louvre.

THE DISTANCE from Calais [A9] to Dover, England, is 41 km and has been swum in less than eight hours.

*The Gothic cathedral **Notre Dame de Paris** [C9] was mainly constructed in the 13th and 14th centuries, but is constantly being restored. The famous Emmanuel bell weighs 13 tonnes.*

ENGLISH CHANNEL

Cherbou
Île d'Ouessant
Brest
St. Malo
Quimper
Laval
Rennes
Lorient
Belle-Île
Angers
St. Nazaire
Nantes
Île d'Yeu
Poitiers
Île de Ré
La Rochelle
BAY OF BISCAY
Cognac
Angoulême
Périgueu
Bordeaux
Dordogne
Bergera
Garonne
Mont-de-Marsan
Agen
Adour
Montauba
Bayonne
Pau
Toulo
Tarbes
Lourdes
PYRENEES
SPAIN
ANDORRA

In the next
...France will provide the UK with enough electricity to power one light bulb in every home.
minute...

8 9 10 11 12 13 14

Calais
Dunkerque
Boulogne
Roubaix
Lille
Lens
Valenciennes
Dieppe
Le Havre
Amiens
St. Quentin
Caen
Rouen
Charleville Mézières
The Seine
BELGIUM

Monaco has a population of only 31,100. The city of **Monte Carlo** is well known for its casinos, harbour, glamour and racetrack.

LUXEM-
BOURG

St. Denis
Versailles **Paris**
Chartres
Fontainebleau
Le Mans
Seine
Marne
Reims
Verdun
Metz
Châlons-en-Champagne
Nancy
Haguenau
Strasbourg
GERMANY

Orléans
Tours
Auxerre
Troyes
Cher
VOSGES
MOUNTAINS

Bourges
Châteauroux
FRANCE
Dijon
Besançon
Saône
Mulhouse

Montluçon
Chalon-sur-Saône
Mâcon
Limoges
JURA
MOUNTAINS
SWITZERLAND

Clermont-Ferrand
Puy de Sancy
1881 m
Bourg-en-Bresse
Chamonix
Mont Blanc
4810 m

ive
Lyon
St. Étienne
Rhône
Chambéry
**MASSIF
CENTRAL**
Tarn
Lot
Valence
Grenoble
ALPS

Montélimar
ITALY

Castres
Nîmes
Avignon
Béziers
Montpellier
Arles
Carcassonne
Sète
Aix-en-Provence
MONACO
Antibes **Monaco**
Marseille
Cannes Nice
rpignan
Toulon St. Tropez
Gulf of Lion

Cape Corse

Bastia

MEDITERRANEAN SEA

Corsica
Gulf of Sagone
Ajaccio

Strait of Bonifacio

0 50 100 150 mi
0 100 200 km

Italy and the Balkans

Northern Italy is highly industrialized and produces many famous brands, such as **Ferrari and Armani, while the south is mainly agricultural.** Croatia, Bosnia and Herzegovina, Serbia, Montenegro, Kosovo and Macedonia were once part of Yugoslavia, but they have each become independent since 1991. Greece is one of Europe's oldest nations. The dry climate, steep slopes and thin soil limit farming to grapes, olives and citrus fruit. This area was home to the ancient Greek and Roman empires, which produced monuments such as Rome's Colosseum and the Parthenon in Athens, as well as Olympia – home to the first Olympic Games in 776 BC.

Facts and Stats

- Italy's population of 60.3 million would fill 603 Olympic stadiums. Montenegro's population of 620,000 would fill six stadiums.

- The life expectancy of people in Italy is 82 years, compared to 75 years in Serbia and a world average of 68 years.

- The average income per person in Italy is £20,940, compared to £1920 in Kosovo and a world average of £5640.

In the next
...Italy will produce over 12,000 packets of pasta – that's 200 km of spaghetti!
minute...

One of the most prominent sights in **Zagreb** [B8], the capital of Croatia, is the cathedral. The spires are 105 m in height and were built after an earthquake in 1880, which damaged much of the original structure.

Did You Know?

It costs the Italian government more money to keep the Tower of Pisa [D5] leaning than it would to straighten it.

SWITZERLAND

AUSTR

Bolzano

SLOVENIA

Aosta

Como
Monza

Lecco
Trento

Udine

Kranj

Ljubljan

Novara
Milan

Bergamo
Brescia Verona

Vicenza
Treviso

Trieste

Kop

Turin

Lodi
Piacenza

Cremona

Padua
Mantua

Venice

Rijeka

Alessandria

Adria

Chioggia

Pula

FRANCE

Parma

Reggio nell'
Emilia

Ferrara

Gulf of
Venice

Genoa
Savona

Bologna

Ravenna

San Remo

La Spezia
Massa
Viareggio

Carrara

Forlì
Pistoia
Prato

Rimini

SAN MARIN
San Marino

Pisa
Livorno

Florence
Empoli

Arezzo

Ancona

Siena

Perugia

ITALY

Elba

Piombino

Grosseto

Terni

Teramo

Civitavecchia

Pesc

Rome

VATICAN CITY
(in Rome)

Latina

Campobasso

Sassari

Gaeta

Benevent

Gulf of
Gaeta

Napl

Nuoro

Salerno

Sardinia

Gulf of
Salerno

Cagliari

TYRRHENIAN SEA

Palermo

Mess

Trapani

Mount Etna
3326 m

Caltanissetta

Agrigento

Catan

Sicily

Ragusa

Sira

Pantelleria

MALTA

Valle

The Grand Canal, Venice [B6], is the main waterway through the city – public transportation is by water, rather than road. Venice is slowly sinking due to rising sea levels. The main squares flood about 60 times a year.

Search and Find

Albania	Malta
• Tiranë F10	• Valletta I7
Bosnia and	**Montenegro**
Herzegovina	• Podgorica E9
• Sarajevo D9	**San Marino**
Croatia	• San Marino . . . D6
• Zagreb B8	**Serbia**
Greece	• Belgrade C10
• Athens H12	**Slovenia**
Italy	• Ljubljana B7
• Rome E6	**Vatican City**
Kosovo	• Vatican City . . . E6
• Pristina E10	
Macedonia	
• Skopje E11	

Maribor
Celje · Varazdin
HUNGARY
vo Mesto · Bjelovar · Subotica
Zagreb · Osijek
Karlovac · Sisak CROATIA
Slavonski Brod · Zrenjanin
Bihac · Prijedor
Banja Luka · Brcko · Bijeljina · Pancevo
BOSNIA AND · Belgrade
spic HERZEGOVINA · Tuzla · Sabac · Smederevo
Zenica · Valjevo
Zadar · Srebrenica · Kragujevac · Negotin
Sarajevo · Uzice · Cacak · Zajecar
Sibenik · Foca · SERBIA · Krusevac
Split Mostar
MONTENEGRO · Novi Pazar · Nis
Ivangrad · Kosovska · Leskovac
Niksic · Mitrovica
Dubrovnik · Podgorica · Pejë · Pristina
Gjakove · Vranje
Cetinje · KOSOVO
Prizren · Kumanovo
Bar · Shkodër · Skopje
MACEDONIA · BULGARIA
Tiranë · Prilep · Drama
Durrës · Lake · Bitola · Kilkis · Sérrai · Xánthi · Komotiní
Elbasan · Ohrid · Florina · Edessa · Kaválla · Alexandroúpolis
ALBANIA · Lake · Ptolemaïs · Thessaloníki · Thásos
Prespa · Veroia · Samothrace
Korçë · Kastoria · Mount Athos
Vlorë · Kozáni · Kateríni · 2033 m
Metéora · Mount Olympus
Ioánnina · 2917 m · Lemnos
Tríkala · Larissa
Corfu · GREECE
Párga · Vólos
Arta · Kardhitsa · Lesbos
Préveza · Lamía
Skíros
Agrínion · Euboea · Chios
Mesalóngion · Thérmon
Pátrai · Thebes · Marathon
Megara · Káristos · Sámos
Piraeus · Athens · Andros · Ikaría
Olympia · Árgos · Tínos
Zákinthos · Kéa · Mykonos
Pyrgos · Páros · Náxos
Peleponnese · Amorgos · Kos
Kalamata · Astipálaia · Rhódes
Neápolis · Rhodes
Kíthira · SEA OF CRETE
Kárpathos
Khaniá · Iráklion
Crete

Bari
Taranto · Brindisi
Lecce
Cosenza
Crotone
Catanzaro
gio di Calabria
IONIAN SEA
Caphalonía
ADRIATIC SEA
oggia

0 50 100 150 200 mi
0 100 200 300 km

THE DISTANCE from the town of Marathon [H12] to Athens [H12] is 42 km, and was first run by a Greek soldier 2500 years ago.

Germany and the Low Countries

Luxembourg, Belgium and the Netherlands are the three nations that make up the low countries.

Much of the Netherlands is below sea level, and it relies on massive sea walls called dykes and thousands of pumps to drain the land. Brussels, the capital of Belgium, is home to the European Union's main centre of government, and Antwerp is the centre of the world's diamond-cutting industry. Luxembourg has the highest income per person in the world due to its banking industry. Germany has the third largest economy in the world after the United States and Japan, and produces machinery and cars such as BMW, Mercedes and Porsche. However, the reunification of East and West Germany in 1990 has caused unemployment and slow economic growth.

Search and Find

Belgium	Luxembourg
• Brussels E5	• Luxembourg. . . G6
Germany	**Netherlands**
• Berlin D11	• Amsterdam . . . D6
	• The Hague. . . . D5

Amsterdam [D6] is well-known for its network of canals. The tall, leaning buildings were once used for storage. Hooks at the top of each house enabled goods to be pulled up to the top rooms.

Map labels

NORTH SEA

Terschelling   Ameland   EA
Vlieland   Waddenzee
Texel   Groning
Den Helder•   Leeuwarden•
NETHERLANDS   •Asse
Alkmaar•   Northeast   Emmen
   Polder
Amsterdam   •Zwolle
Haarlem•   Flevoland
Leiden•   Polder   Apeldoorn
The Hague   •Hilversum
   Utrecht•   Enschede•
Delft•   •Gouda   •Arnhem
Rotterdam•   Waal Nijmegen•
Dordrecht•   Müns
Vlissingen•   •Breda   Tilburg• 's-Hertogenbosch
Zeebrugge•   Maas (Meuse)
Ostend•   •Bruges   Eindhoven•   Dortmu
Ghent•   •Antwerp   Duisburg•   •Esser
Roeselare•   Aalst•   •Mechelen   Krefeld•   Wuppe
Kortrijk•   Leuven•   Genk•   Düsseldorf•   Solingen•
   Hasselt•   •Maastricht   •Cologn
Brussels   •Aachen
Tournai•   Namur•   •Liège   •Bonn
Charleroi•   •Verviers
Mons•   Meuse (Maas)   •Dinant
FRANCE   **BELGIUM**   HUNSRÜCK   Rhine
   Bastogne•   Kobler
LUXEMBOURG   W
Luxembourg   •Trier
Esch-sur-Alzette•
   Saarbrücken•   Kaiserslaut
FRANCE
   Karlsru
   Baden-Ba
   B
   F
   Freiburg
   im Breis
   SW

Scale: 0   50   100   150   200 mi
0   100   200   300 km

Facts and Stats

• Germany's population of 82.8 million would fill 828 Olympic stadiums. Luxembourg's population of 484,000 would only fill 4.8 stadiums.

• Mount Zugspitze [I9] is the highest mountain at 2964 m – nine times higher than the Eiffel Tower.

• The average income per person in Luxembourg is £29,600, compared to a world average of £5640.

COLOGNE [E7] holds one of the biggest carnivals in the world. Every November, more than one million people take part in the festival.

THE DISTANCE from the source of the Rhine river [F7] in the Swiss Alps to its mouth at the North Sea is 1320 km.

8 9 10 11 12 13 14

A

Sylt
DENMARK
Flensburg
Schleswig
Kiel Bay
Fehmarn
Kiel
Mecklenburg
Bay
Rügen

B

SIAN ISLANDS
Cuxhaven
Lübeck
Rostock
Greifswald
helmshaven
Bremerhaven
Hamburg
Schwerin
Idenburg
Bremen
Lüneburg
Neubrandenburg

C

Ems
nabrück
Hannover
Wolfsburg
Brandenburg
Berlin
Elbe
Bielefeld
Braunschweig
Potsdam
Hameln
Magdeburg
Frankfurt an der Oder
POLAND

D

Hamm
Paderborn
Dessau
Cottbus
Göttingen
Kassel
Halle
GERMANY
Leipzig
Elbe

E

iegen
Eisenach
Weimar
Meissen
Görlitz
Erfurt
Giessen
Jena
Chemnitz
Dresden
Fulda
Gera
Freital
Zwickau

F

len
Frankfurt am Main
Plauen
Offenbach
CZECH REPUBLIC
Mainz
Darmstadt
Main
orms
Bamberg
nnheim
Würzburg
Bayreuth

G

wigshafen
eidelberg
Fürth
Nuremberg
Heilbronn
BOHEMIAN FOREST

H

Pforzheim
Regensburg
Stuttgart
Tübingen
Ingolstadt
Reutlingen
Passau
SWABIAN JURA
Ulm
Augsburg

I

Danube
Munich
Lake
Constance
BAVARIAN ALPS
Mount Zugspitze
2964 m
Berchtesgaden

J

LAND
AUSTRIA

8 9 10 11 12 13 14

Did You Know?

Each year, Belgium produces and sells 172,000 tonnes of chocolate in more than 2130 chocolate shops.

In the next

...the Netherlands will make 1280 kg of cheese – enough for 64,000 cheese slices.

minute...

World Record

Germany has the highest paper recycling rate in the world – more than 75 percent of their paper is reused.

Cologne Cathedral [E7] is one of the tallest and most magnificent Gothic buildings in the world. Its construction began in the 13th century, but wasn't completed until the late 19th century. The cathedral has 12 bells, and 509 steps lead to the top of the south tower, nearly 100 m above the ground.

Switzerland and Austria

Landlocked Switzerland, Austria and Liechtenstein are dominated by the Alps, creating stunning mountain scenery. Millions of tourists are attracted to the natural beauty, spectacular mountain vistas and popular Alpine skiing. Switzerland guards its independence and was not involved in either of the two World Wars. As a neutral, independent state, Switzerland is part of the United Nations and many charitable and banking organizations. As a result, it is a very wealthy country. Many composers come from Austria, including Mozart, Haydn, Schubert and Strauss.

▷ **The Belvedere Palace,** Vienna [E13], was built in the 17th and 18th centuries. Archduke Franz Ferdinand was the last person to live at the palace. It is now a museum and gallery, exhibiting many important collections, including the works of Renoir, Monet and Van Gogh.

In the next ...41,000 kg of chocolate will be eaten worldwide. The Swiss are the world's biggest consumers. **minute...**

Schaffhausen

Basel · Rhine
Aarau · Baden · Winterthur · Lake Constance · GERMANY
FRANCE · Olten · Solothurn · Zürich
Biel · St. Gallen · Bregenz
Neuchâtel · Zug · Feldkirch · Innsbruck
Lake Neuchâtel · Bern · Lucerne · SWITZERLAND · Vaduz · LIECHTENSTEIN
Yverdon · Thun · LIECHTENSTEIN · St. Anton
Fribourg · Interlaken · Chur · Galtür
Lausanne · Saanen · Andermatt · LEPONTINE ALPS · Davos
Lake Geneva · Montreux · BERNESE ALPS
Geneva · Sion · Brig · St. Moritz
Zermatt · Mount Dufourspitze 4634 m · Bellinzona
Mount Matterhorn 4478 m · Locarno · ITALY
ITALY · Lugano

Did You Know?

The Swiss invented the quartz watch, wristwatch and waterproof watch. Switzerland produces expensive watches, such as Rolex, and watch-making is its third largest industry.

▷ **Leukerbad,** in the heart of the Bernese Alps [G3], is the largest thermal spa in Europe. Dating back to Roman times, the complex contains 3.9 million litres of water and is surrounded by picturesque mountain scenery.

BERN [F3] is the city where Albert Einstein worked, the Toblerone chocolate bar is made, and Emmental cheese is manufactured.

THE DISTANCE of the St. Moritz [G5] bobsleigh run is 1585 m and it takes just 70 seconds to travel from one end to the other.

Search and Find

Austria
- Vienna E13

Liechtenstein
- Vaduz F5

Switzerland
- Bern F3

Extreme Weather

In 1999, the biggest avalanche in Austria for 400 years smashed into the town of Galtür [G6], killing 31 people.

| 0 | 50 | 100 mi |
| 0 | 80 | 160 km |

CZECH REPUBLIC

SLOVAKIA

Zwettl Stadt

Inn

Braunau

Linz

Krems

Danube

Wels

Amstetten

Klosterneuburg

Steyr

Sankt Pölten

Vienna

Gmunden

Salzburg

Baden

Hallein

Bad Ischl

Wiener Neustadt

Neusiedler See

Kufstein

AUSTRIA

Schwaz

Kitzbühel

Mount Grossglockner 3797 m

Leoben

Kapfenberg

HOHE TAUERN

NIEDERE TAUERN

Knittelfeld

Judenburg

Mur

HUNGARY

Graz

Gleisdorf

Spittal

Wolfsberg

ITALY

Drau

Villach

Klagenfurt

SLOVENIA

Facts and Stats

- The population of Liechtenstein is only 36,100 and wouldn't even fill half an Olympic stadium.

- Switzerland's Mount Dufourspitze [H3] is the highest mountain at 4634 m in height – 14 times higher than the Eiffel Tower.

- The average income per person in Switzerland is £42,570 compared to a world average of £5640.

▷ Switzerland is split into federal states, or cantons. Bern is the second largest Swiss canton, and is dominated by mountains, glaciers and waterfalls. The small village of **Gstaad** near Saanen [G2] is a popular ski resort with fantastic Alpine scenery.

Hungary, Romania and Bulgaria

Bulgaria and Romania became members of the European Union in 2007, with Hungary joining in 2004. These countries will now experience rapid economic growth after decades of communist rule. Romania is the largest of the three and Europe's longest river, the Danube, flows along its southern border to the Black Sea. Hungary's capital, Budapest, has a lively arts and music scene, and is host to a range of cultural and sporting festivals. The countryside is scenic with many lakes, historic towns and villages. Bulgaria also borders the Black Sea, but it is mainly mountainous and rural, and relatively undeveloped.

SLOVAKIA

AUSTRIA

Miskolc

Gyor

Esztergom

Budapest

Szombathely

HUNGARY

Székesfehérvár

SLOVENIA

Lake Balaton

Dunaujvaros

Kecskemét

Kaposvár

Tisza

Szeged

Arad

CROATIA

Danube

Pécs

Timisoara

SERBIA

Facts and Stats

• The Danube [D6/G10] is the longest river at 2860 km in length. The Nile river is twice as long.

• Mount Musala [I10] is the highest mountain at 2925 m, which is nine times higher than the Eiffel Tower.

• The average income per person in Hungary is £8000, compared to a world average of £5640.

▷ *On the bank of the Danube river in Budapest [C6] is **Hungary's Parliament building**. Hungarian architect, Imre Steindl, designed the building, although he went blind before the project was completed. More than 40 kg of gold was used in its construction.*

◁ ***Bran Castle** in Romania is more commonly known as Dracula's Castle because Bram Stoker based his novel around the building. In 2007, the castle was put up for sale for £40 million.*

Did You Know?

One of the few Bulgarian commercial crops is the rose. The petals are used in the perfume industry.

THE DISTANCE from the source to the mouth of the Danube river [D6/G10] is 2888 km – almost all of it is accessible to boats.

ESZTERGOM [C5] is a former capital of Hungary and home to the nation's largest church, the Esztergom Basilica.

Search and Find

Bulgaria
● Sofia I9
Hungary
● Budapest C6

Romania
● Bucharest . . . F11

In the next ...61,000 litres of water will enter the Black Sea from the Danube river. **minute...**

UKRAINE

Nyíregyháza

● Satu Mare

Debrecen

● Baia Mare

● Oradea

Suceava ●

Iasi ●

MOLDOVA

● Cluj-Napoca

● Bacău

● Târgu Mures

UKRAINE

ROMANIA

Mures

Alba Iulia ●

Olt

Sibiu ●

Brasov ●

Focsani ●

Galati ●
Braila ●

CARPATHIAN MOUNTAINS

TRANSYLVANIAN ALPS

● Tulcea

Resita

● Ploiesti

Pitesti ●

● Bucharest

Calarasi ●

Constanta ●

● Drobeta-Turnu Severin

● Craiova

Giurgiu ●

● Ruse

Dobrich ●

Vidin ●

Jiu

Danube

SERBIA

Montana ●

● Pleven

Shumen ●

Varna ●

BULGARIA

Iskur

Vratsa ●

Gabrovo ●

BLACK
SEA

BALKAN MOUNTAINS

Sliven ●

Burgas ●

Pernik ●

● **Sofia**

Stara Zagora ●

● Yambol

Mount Musala
2925 m

Kyustendil ●

Plovdiv ●

Dimitrovgrad ●

Blagoevgrad ●

RHODOPE MOUNTAINS

Khaskovo ●

Maritsa

TURKEY

MACEDONIA

Struma

GREECE

0   50   100 mi
0   80   160 km

Poland, Czech Republic and Slovakia

Poland, Slovakia and the Czech Republic are among the newest members of the European Union. Standards of living are much lower than western Europe and many workers have moved to the United Kingdom and Ireland for better-paid jobs. However, since joining the EU, Slovakia has become a major car producer, and has seen minimal emigration. The Baltic coast of Poland is industrial with steelworks and shipyards, but low-wage rates and money from the EU have attracted new industries. Prague, the capital of the Czech Republic, is situated on the Vltava river and receives more than ten million tourists a year.

The **Prague Astronomical Clock** [G5] is mounted on the wall of the Old Town City Hall. The astronomical dial represents the Sun and Moon. The 12 figures of the Apostles appear every hour, and all 12 are seen at 12 p.m. Finally, the calendar dial represents the months.

In the next ...Poland will mine 190 tonnes of coal, generating enough electricity for 7.6 million light bulbs. minute...

Zygmunt's Column sits in the centre of **Castle Square, Warsaw** [E10]. Built in 1644, the monument represents King Zygmunt III Waza. Markets, street entertainment and concerts take place here, making it a popular tourist site.

BALTIC SEA

Koszalin

Szczecin

Notéc

Gorzow Wielkopolski

Warta

Poznar

Zielona Gora

Kali

Oder

Legnica

Wroclav

Opole

Walbrzych

GERMANY

Liberec

Ústí nad Labem

Hradec Kralove

Karlovy Vary

Cheb

Prague

Elbe

Pardubice

Plzen

CZECH REPUBLIC

Olomouc

Jihlava

BOHEMIAN FOREST

Vltava

Zlir

Brno

Ceské Budejovice

Morava

AUSTRIA

Trenc

Trnava

Bratislava

Komárr

8 9 10 11 12 13 14

A
B
C
D
E
F
G
H
I
J

0 50 100 mi
0 80 160 km

Gulf of Danzig

KALININGRAD (RUSSIAN FEDERATION)

LITHUANIA

BELARUS

• Gdynia

Gdansk

• Elblag

Suwalki •

Vistula

• Olsztyn

Bydgoszcz

• Torun

Narew

Bialystok •

Vloclawek •

Bug

• Plock

● **Warsaw**

POLAND

Lodz •

Pilica

• Radom

• Lublin

Chelm •

• Czestochowa

Vistula

San

Bytom
• Sosnowiece
wice •
• Katowice

• Rzeszow

Auschwitz ◆
strava
• Bielsko-Biala
• Kraków
• Wieliczka
• Tarnow

UKRAINE

Gerlachovsky Stit 2655 m

ah
• Zilina

• Poprad

Martin •
• Presov

TATRA MOUNTAINS

Kosice •

ojnice
•
• Banská Bystrica

SLOVAKIA

tra
• Levice

HUNGARY

ube

Search and Find

Czech Republic
● Prague G5
Poland
● Warsaw E10

Slovakia
● Bratislava J7

AUSCHWITZ [G8] was the centre of the Holocaust mass killings. Now a World Heritage site, it has 700,000 visitors a year.

THE DISTANCE across the Charles Bridge, Prague [G5] is 516 m. The bridge is lined with 30 statues dating from around 1700.

Facts and Stats

• The longest river is the Vistula river [G10] at 1047 km in length – six times shorter than the Nile river.

• The highest mountain is Gerlachovsky Stit [H9] at 2655 m – eight times higher than the Eiffel Tower.

• The average income per person in Poland is £7560, compared to a world average of £5640.

Did You Know?

Under the town of Wieliczka [G9] is one of the oldest salt mines in the world. The mine is so large that it has passages, lakes, buildings and a church. It is now a popular tourist attraction.

▷ *Bojnice Castle [I8] is the most visited Slovakian castle, attracting more than 200,000 visitors a year. Many films have been shot here and the International Festival of Ghosts and Monsters takes place every spring.*

Eastern Europe

The former Soviet states of Estonia, Latvia and Lithuania are now **democratic, independent countries**. The area is mainly flat, low-lying land that is covered in snow during winter, but a fertile grain- and dairy-farming region in summer. Without industries to compete with western Europe, these countries remain poor. Russia controls much of Europe's natural gas supplies, but has struggled to improve its standard of living. Armenia, Azerbaijan and Georgia are part of the Caucasus range with the Caucasus Mountains providing a border between Europe and Asia.

*The town of Trakai, Lithuania, can be found west of Vilnius [G5]. Out of the area's 200 lakes, Lake Galve is the largest at 47 m in depth. Built in the 14th and 15th centuries on the lake, **Trakai Island Castle** can only be reached by a drawbridge.*

Search and Find

Armenia
- Yerevan J8

Azerbaijan
- Baku J9

Belarus
- Minsk G6

Estonia
- Tallinn E5

Georgia
- Thilisi I8

Latvia
- Riga F5

Lithuania
- Vilnius G5

Moldova
- Chisinau H6

Russian Federation
- Moscow F7

Ukraine
- Kiev G6

*A kremlin is a Russian castle, the most famous is the **Moscow Kremlin** [F7] on the bank of the Moskva river. Surrounded by a wall, the Kremlin includes four palaces, four golden-domed cathedrals and 20 towers.*

In the next minute...
...Russia will sell enough natural gas to Europe to light 250 million gas fires.

BARENT

FINLAND

Murmansk

Onega

Lake Onega

Petrozavo

Vyborg

Lake Ladoga

St. Petersburg

Gulf of Finland

Tallinn

ESTONIA

Tartu

Lake Peipus

Novgorod

Rybinsk

Yaroslav

Tver

BALTIC SEA

Gulf of Riga

Liepaja

Riga

LATVIA

Vitsyebsk

Moscow

RUSSIAN FEDERATION

LITHUANIA

Vilnius

BELARUS

Smolensk

Ryazar

Kaliningrad

Kaunas

Minsk

Kirov

T

POLAND

Hrodna

Bryansk

Homyel

Lipets

Pripyat Marshes

Voronezh

Rivne

Kiev

Dnieper

Lviv

UKRAINE

Khark

SLOVAKIA

Dnipropetrovsi

Prut

Kryvyy Rih

Donetsk

MOLDOVA

Dniester

Zaporizhzhya

Rostov na-Do

Chisinau

ROMANIA

Tiraspol

Odessa

Sea of Azov

Crimea

Krasnod

Sevastopol

BLACK SEA

ARCTIC
OCEAN

Novaya Zemlya

KARA SEA

Kolguyev Island

Vorkuta •

Pechora

khangelísk

Severnaya Dvina

Ukhta •

• Syktyvkar

**RUSSIAN
FEDERATION**

U R A L   M O U N T A I N S

• Perm

• Izhevsk

Nizhniy Novgorod
• Kazan

• Ufa

Simbirsk
Tolyatti
• Penza   Samara
Orenburg
Ural
Orsk •
Magnitogorsk •

Saratov

Volga

KAZAKHSTAN

• Volgograd

• Astrakhan

CASPIAN SEA

Stavropol
• Vladikavkaz
• Grozny
unt Elbrus 5642 m
EORGIA
Tbilisi
RMENIA
Yerevan   • Baku
AZERBAIJAN
IRAN

Extreme Weather

For seven months, the far north of Russia has temperatures below freezing and only two months above 10°C. It is too cold even for trees to grow.

Facts and Stats

• The population of Russia is 142.9 million and would fill 1429 Olympic stadiums. It is more than 100 times larger than Estonia's population of 1.3 million.

• Russia's area is 17 million km² – 165 times the area of Iceland. It is the biggest country in the world.

• The average income per person in Moldova is £990, compared to £9500 in Estonia and a world average of £5640.

THE DISTANCE from Vilnius [G5] to Tallinn [E5] was once covered by two million citizens in a human chain stretching more than 300 km.

ST. PETERSBURG [E6] has many canals and hundreds of bridges. It is sometimes called the Venice of the North.

Did You Know?

The region contains three states, which have declared independence: Transnistria (eastern Moldova) and Abkhazia and South Ossetia (regions of Georgia). These states are independent in practice but go largely unrecognised.

0	100	200	300	400	500 mi
0	200	400	600	800 km	

*Matryoshka are brightly painted wooden **Russian dolls**. They are made in such a way that they can be taken apart to reveal smaller dolls that fit inside one another.*

Africa

TUNISIA

MOROCCO

ALGERIA

LIBYA

EGYPT

MAURITANIA

CAPE VERDE

MALI

NIGER

SUDAN

ERITREA

SENEGAL

1

2

BURKINA
FASO

CHAD

9

GUINEA

6

NIGERIA

CENTRAL
AFRICAN
REPUBLIC

SOUTH
SUDAN

ETHIOPIA

3

COTE
D'IVOIRE

5

4

LIBERIA

CAMEROON

SÃO TOMÉ
AND PRÍNCIPE

7

DEMOCRATIC
REPUBLIC OF
THE CONGO

UGANDA

SOMALIA

SEYCHELLES

GABON

KENYA

8

10

INDIAN
OCEAN

11

ATLANTIC
OCEAN

TANZANIA

COMOROS

ANGOLA

ZAMBIA

MALAWI

MOZAMBIQUE

MAURITIUS

NAMIBIA

ZIMBABWE

BOTSWANA

MADAGASCAR

12

13

SOUTH
AFRICA

KEY
1 GAMBIA
2 GUINEA-BISSAU
3 SIERRA LEONE
4 GHANA
5 TOGO
6 BENIN
7 EQUATORIAL GUINEA
8 REPUBLIC OF THE CONGO
9 DJIBOUTI
10 RWANDA
11 BURUNDI
12 SWAZILAND
13 LESOTHO

COUNTRY FACTFILE

Country	Life expectancy	Population in thousands	Population growth %	Population as urban %	Literacy %	Area km²	Population density per km²	Capital city	Currency	Languages
Algeria	75	34,080	1.2	66	70	2,381,741	14.3	Algiers	Algerian Dinar	Arabic, Berber, French
Angola	55	20,609	2	59	67	1,246,700	16.5	Luanda	Kwanza	Portuguese, Umbundu
Benin	60	8850	2.9	43	35	112,622	78.6	Porto-Novo, Cotonou	CFA Franc	French, Fon, Yoruba
Botswana	56	2038	1.7	66	81	581,730	3.5	Gaborone	Pula	English, Tswana
Burkina Faso	54	15,225	3.1	26	22	274,122	55.5	Ouagadougou	CFA Franc	French, Mossi
Burundi	59	8039	3.5	11	39	27,834	288.8	Bujumbura	Burundi Franc	Kirundi, French
Cameroon	55	19,406	2.2	58	68	476,077	40.8	Yaoundé	CFA Franc	French, English, Fang
Cape Verde	71	492	1.4	62	77	4033	122	Praia	Cape Verdean Escudo	Portuguese, Crioulo
Central African Republic	50	4400	2.1	42	49	622,436	7.1	Bangui	CFA Franc	French, Sangho
Chad	48	11,176	2	28	26	1,284,000	8.7	N'Djamena	CFA Franc	French, Arabic, Sara
Comoros	63	669	2.7	32	57	1862	359.3	Moroni	Comoran Franc	Comorian, French, Arabic
Congo, Democratic Republic of the	56	66,000	2.6	35	66	2,344,856	28.1	Kinshasa	Congolese Franc	French, Lingala, Swahili
Congo, Republic of the	55	4002	2.8	63	84	342,000	11.7	Brazzaville	CFA Franc	French, Monokutuba, Kongo
Côte d'Ivoire (Ivory Coast)	57	20,080	2.1	51	49	320,783	62.5	Yamoussoukro, Abidjan	CFA Franc	French, Akan
Djibouti	62	818	2.2	85	68	23,200	35.3	Djibouti	Djiboutian Franc	Somali, French, Akan
Egypt	73	77,775	1.9	45	71	997,739	78	Cairo	Egyptian Pound	Arabic
Equatorial Guinea	63	700	2.6	48	87	28,051	25	Malabo	CFA Franc	Spanish, French, Fang
Eritrea	63	5291	2.5	22	59	121,100	43.7	Asmara	Nakfa	Tigrinya, Arabic, Afar
Ethiopia	57	82,102	3.2	18	43	1,127,127	72.8	Addis Ababa	Birr	Amharic, Oromo, Tigrinya
Gabon	52	1505	1.9	86	63	267,667	5.6	Libreville	CFA Franc	French, Fang
Gambia	64	1660	2.4	58	40	10,689	155.3	Banjul	Dalasi	English, Malinke
Ghana	61	24,223	1.8	51	58	238,533	101.5	Accra	Cedi	Hausa, English, Akan
Guinea	59	10,218	2.6	35	36	245,857	41.6	Conakry	Guinean Franc	Fulani, French, Malinke
Guinea-Bissau	49	1521	2	30	42	36,125	42.1	Bissau	CFA Franc	Crioulo, Portuguese, Balante
Kenya	63	38,611	2.5	30	85	582,646	66.3	Nairobi	Kenyan Shilling	Swahili, English, Kikuyu
Lesotho	62	2170	0.3	27	85	30,355	71.5	Maseru	Loti	Sesotho, English
Liberia	57	3990	3.7	60	58	111,370	35.8	Monrovia	US Dollar, Liberian Dollar	Krio, English
Libya	78	6355	2.1	88	83	1,777,060	3.6	Tripoli	Libyan Dinar	Arabic
Madagascar	64	20,696	3	30	69	587,041	35.3	Antananarivo	Madagascar Ariary	Malagasy, French
Malawi	52	14,389	2.8	20	63	118,484	121.4	Lilongwe	Malawian Kwacha	Chichewa, English
Mali	53	14,529	2.6	36	46	1,248,574	11.6	Bamako	CFA Franc	French, Bambara
Mauritania	62	3162	2.3	58	51	1,030,700	3.1	Nouakchott	Ouguiya	Arabic
Mauritius	75	1281	0.7	48	84	2040	627.9	Port Louis	Mauritius Rupee	French Creole, Bhojpuri, English
Morocco	76	31,950	1.1	58	52	446,550	71.5	Rabat	Moroccan Dirham	Arabic, Berber
Mozambique	52	23,300	2.4	38	48	801,590	29.1	Maputo	Metical	Emakhuwa, Portuguese
Namibia	52	2125	0.9	38	85	824,269	2.6	Windhoek	Namibian Dollar	English, Ovambo, Nama
Niger	54	15,731	3.6	21	29	1,186,408	13.3	Niamey	CFA Franc	French, Hausa
Nigeria	52	140,432	1.9	50	68	923,103	152.1	Abuja	Naira	English, Hausa, Yoruba
Rwanda	58	9500	2.8	18	70	26,338	360.7	Kigali	Rwandan Franc	Rwanda, French, English
São Tomé and Príncipe	63	152	2.1	62	85	1001	151.8	São Tomé	Dobra	Portuguese, Crioulo
Senegal	60	12,179	2.6	47	40	196,712	61.9	Dakar	CFA Franc	French, Wolof, Fulani
Seychelles	74	90.9	0.9	59	92	455	199.8	Victoria	Seychelles Rupee	Creole, English
Sierra Leone	57	5870	2.2	38	35	71,740	81.8	Freetown	Leone	English, Krio, Mende
Somalia	50	9300	1.6	37	38	637,657	14.6	Mogadishu	Somali Shilling	Somali, Arabic
South Africa	49	49,900	0.0	62	86	1,224,691	40.7	Pretoria, Cape Town	Rand	Xhosa, English, Zulu, Afrikaans
South Sudan	n/a	8,260	2	22	n/a	619,745	13.3	Juba	South Sudanese Pound	English, Dinka, Arabic
Sudan	63	30,894	2.1	40	60	1,886,070	16.4	Khartoum	Sudanese Dinar	Arabic, Nubian
Swaziland	49	1018	1.2	34	82	17,363	58.6	Mbabane, Lobamba	Lilangeni	Swazi, English
Tanzania	53	44,800	2	26	69	945,037	47.4	Dar es Salaam, Dodoma	Tanzanian Shilling	Swahili, English
Togo	63	6191	2.8	43	61	56,785	109	Lomé	CFA Franc	French, Ewe
Tunisia	76	10,674	1	67	75	163,610	65.2	Tunis	Tunisian Dinar	Arabic, French
Uganda	53	31,785	3.6	14	66	241,040	131.9	Kampala	Ugandan Shilling	Swahili, English, Ganda
Zambia	53	13,047	3.1	44	81	752,614	17.3	Lusaka	Zambian Kwacha	English, Bemba
Zimbabwe	52	12,500	4.3	38	90	390,757	31.9	Harare	Zimbabwean Dollar	English, Shona

North Africa

The Sahara Desert dominates this region at 6000 km in width and 2000 km from north to south. Only a narrow strip of land stands next to the Mediterranean Sea, but the fertile valleys of the Atlas Mountains and the banks of the Nile river have enough water to grow crops.

Algeria, Libya and Tunisia have become wealthy by selling oil and natural gas to Europe. Egypt was the richest country in the world when the pharaohs ruled more than 3000 years ago. Egypt's well-preserved tombs and temples, especially the Great Pyramid of Giza, attract many tourists.

Strait of Gibraltar

Tangier
CEUTA (SPAIN)
Tétouan
MELILLA (SPAIN)

ATLANTIC OCEAN

Kénitra
Rabat
Casablanca
Fes
Meknès
Oujda

Safi
MOROCCO

Marrakech
Mount Toubkal 4176 m
Agadir

Sidi Ifni
ATLAS MOUNTAINS

Tarfaya

WESTERN SAHARA

Tindouf

MAURITANIA

Ech-Cheliff
Oran
Sidi Bel Abbès

Algiers
Blida
Bejaïa
Constantine
Batna

Skikda
Annaba
Bizerte
Tunis
Nabe
Souss
Kairouan

TELL ATLAS

SAHARAN ATLAS MOUNTAINS

Ghardaïa

Béchar

ALGERIA

TUNISIA

Sfa

Ghadam

Adrar

In Salah

AHAGGAR

Tahat Peak 2918 m

Tamanrasset

MALI

S A H A R A

D E S

NIGER

Did You Know?

The Sahara Desert region was wet and fertile 8000 years ago. As the climate has become drier, the desert has expanded.

◁ In north Africa, many civilizations live in fortified cities, or ksars. **Aït Benhaddou** is situated near Marrakech [E2], Morocco. Few familes live here now as they have moved to modern villages nearby. Scenes from films including Alexander (2004) and The Mummy (1999) have been shot here.

In the next ...the Sun will evaporate the equivalent of 110 million bottles of water from the Nile river. minute...

▷ Located on the Nile river, Cairo [F13] is the biggest city in Africa. Built in AD 988, **Al-Azhar University** is the second oldest university in the world, after the University of Al Karaouine Fez, Morocco. Al-Azhar Mosque stands alongside the university.

Facts and Stats

• Egypt's population of 77.8 million would fill 778 Olympic stadiums. Libya's population of 6.4 million would only fill 64 stadiums.

• Cairo [F13] is the biggest city with 15.5 million people. This would fill 155 Olympic stadiums, compared to Tripoli which would only fill 14 [E8].

• The average income per person in Libya is £7140, compared to a world average of £5640.

Search and Find

Algeria
• Algiers C6
Egypt
• Cairo F13
Libya
• Tripoli E8

Morocco
• Rabat D3
Tunisia
• Tunis D7

World Record

The Sahara sand sea in Algeria has the longest sand dunes in the world, with some more than 300 km.

Extreme Weather

The hottest temperature ever recorded was 58°C in Libya's Sahara Desert.

MEDITERRANEAN SEA

Tripoli
Misurata
-Zawiyah
Darnah
Gulf of Sidra
Benghazi
Tubruq
Surt
Port Said
Alexandria
Tanta
Suez Canal
Ajdabiya
Cairo
Suez
QATTARA DEPRESSION
Giza
Sinai Peninsula
ISRAEL
GREAT SAND SEA
Nile
Gulf of Suez
LIBYA
LIBYAN DESERT
WESTERN DESERT
Sharm al Sheikh
El Minya
Al Ghardaqah
Asyut
RED SEA
Gulf of Aqaba
abha
FEZZAN
EGYPT
Qena
Luxor
T
Aswan
GILF KEBIR PLATEAU
Lake Nasser
CHAD
SUDAN

THE DISTANCE separating Morocco from Spain, Europe, at the Strait of Gibraltar's [C3] narrowest point is only 13 km.

EGYPT has huge pyramids, built more than 3000 years ago. Each one held the body of a king.

▷ **Desert tribe people,** such as the Berbers and Tuaregs, travel by camel from oasis to oasis across the Sahara Desert to trade cloth, salt and spices.

West Africa

Stretching from the heart of the Sahara Desert to the tropical forests of southern Nigeria, this region is one of the poorest in the world. In the north, Mali and Niger are plagued by drought and famine. The southern countries of Sierra Leone, Liberia, Côte d'Ivoire and Nigeria suffer with armed unrest, government corruption and civil wars. Oil provides 65 percent of Nigeria's income, but this fails to lift the rapidly growing population out of poverty.

Extreme Weather

Southern Nigeria has eight times as much rain as London. However, parts of northern Mali have almost no rain.

CANARY ISLANDS (SPAIN)

Las Palmas de Gran Canaria

MOROCCO

El Aaiún

WESTERN SAHARA

ALGERIA

Dakhla

Zouérat

SAHARA

MAURITANIA

MALI

Mindelo

CAPE VERDE

Nouadhibou

Nouakchott

Tombouctou

Senegal

Praia

St. Louis

Kaédi

Mopti

Touba

Djenné

Dakar

Thiès

SENEGAL

Kayes

Ségou

Banjul

GAMBIA

Ouagadoug

ATLANTIC OCEAN

Bamako

GUINEA-BISSAU

Bissau

BURKIN

GUINEA

Sikasso

Conakry

Kankan

Bobo Dioulasso

Freetown

SIERRA LEONE

COTE D'IVOIRE

Tamale

Bo

Man

Bouaké

Monrovia

Harbel

Daloa

Kumasi

Yamoussoukro

GHAN

Buchanan

Abidjan

Accra

LIBERIA

Sekondi-Takor

Cape Palmas

GULF

| 0 | 100 | 200 | 300 | 400 mi |
| 0 | 200 | 400 | 600 km |

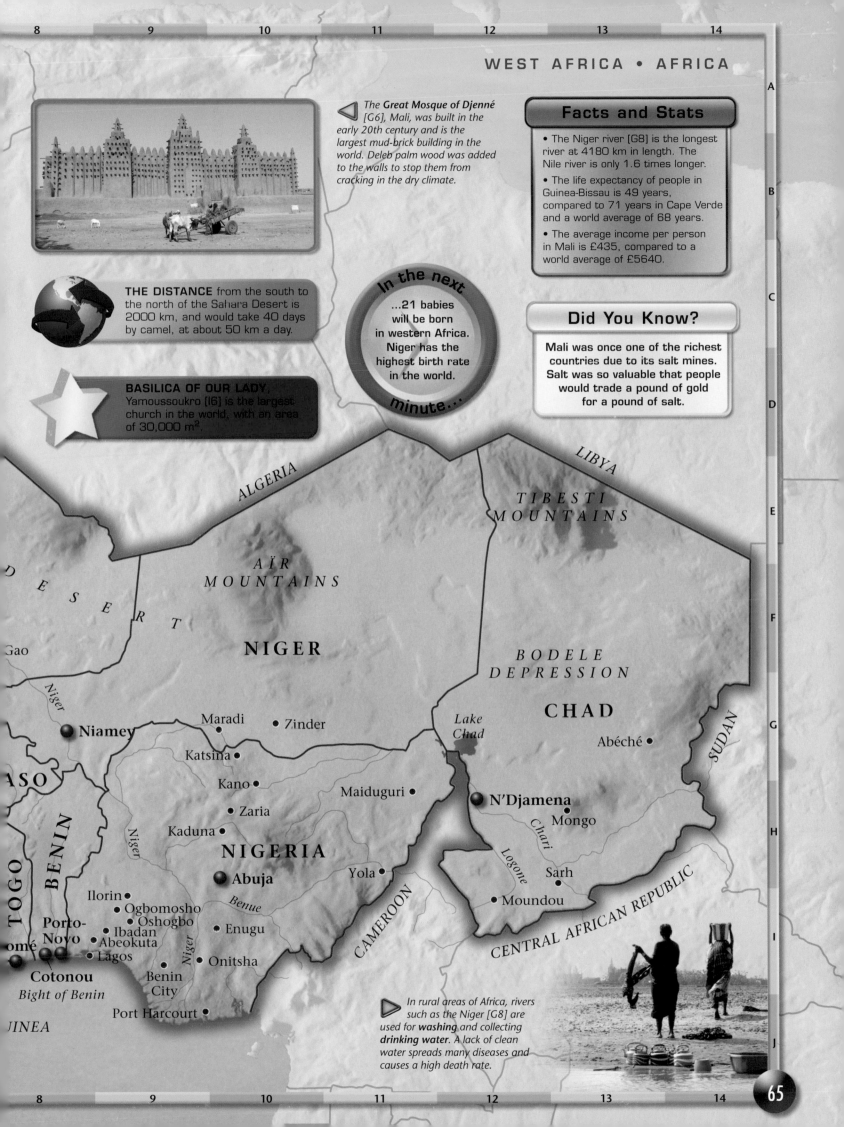

The **Great Mosque of Djenné** [G6], Mali, was built in the early 20th century and is the largest mud-brick building in the world. Deleb palm wood was added to the walls to stop them from cracking in the dry climate.

Facts and Stats

• The Niger river [G8] is the longest river at 4180 km in length. The Nile river is only 1.6 times longer.

• The life expectancy of people in Guinea-Bissau is 49 years, compared to 71 years in Cape Verde and a world average of 68 years.

• The average income per person in Mali is £435, compared to a world average of £5640.

THE DISTANCE from the south to the north of the Sahara Desert is 2000 km, and would take 40 days by camel, at about 50 km a day.

In the next
...21 babies will be born in western Africa. Niger has the highest birth rate in the world.
minute...

Did You Know?

Mali was once one of the richest countries due to its salt mines. Salt was so valuable that people would trade a pound of gold for a pound of salt.

BASILICA OF OUR LADY, Yamoussoukro [I6] is the largest church in the world, with an area of 30,000 m².

ALGERIA

LIBYA

TIBESTI MOUNTAINS

AÏR MOUNTAINS

DESERT

Gao

NIGER

BODELE DEPRESSION

CHAD

Niger

Maradi

Zinder

Lake Chad

Abéché

SUDAN

● Niamey

Katsina

Kano

Maiduguri

● N'Djamena

Zaria

Mongo

ASO

Niger

Kaduna

NIGERIA

Chari

Logone

TOGO

BENIN

● Abuja

Yola

Sarh

Ilorin

Benue

CAMEROON

● Moundou

Ogbomosho

Oshogbo

Enugu

CENTRAL AFRICAN REPUBLIC

Porto-Novo

Ibadan

Abeokuta

Niger

omé

Lagos

Onitsha

Cotonou

Benin City

Bight of Benin

Port Harcourt

JINEA

In rural areas of Africa, rivers such as the Niger [G8] are used for **washing** and collecting **drinking water**. A lack of clean water spreads many diseases and causes a high death rate.

East Africa

Due to the high altitude of Kenya, Tanzania and Uganda, the climate is suited to growing crops. These countries have strong economies based on exporting crops, such as tea and coffee, which are grown on large plantations run by European companies. Kenya also has a strong tourist industry as people visit to see animals in their natural habitat. The countries of Ethiopia, Somalia and Sudan are poorer as they have harsher climates and a history of civil war. The droughts that have repeatedly affected this southern fringe of the Sahara Desert have caused millions of deaths as well as the destruction of crops and animals.

Lesser flamingos are the smallest of the flamingo family. They are numerous throughout Africa and are always found in large groups called 'pats'. The colour of flamingos comes from their food – unhealthy birds are pale in colour.

Facts and Stats

• Mount Kilimanjaro [H9] is the highest mountain at 5895 m. It is 18 times higher than the Eiffel Tower.

• Sudan's area is 1.9 million km². This is 18 times the area of Iceland.

• Ethiopia has a population of 82.1 million. This would fill 821 Olympic stadiums. Djibouti's population is 818,000 and would only fill 8 Olympic stadiums.

Extreme Weather

The Danakil Valley [D10], Ethiopia, has the hottest average daily temperature of 55°C.

Did You Know?

Somaliland declared itself independent from Somalia in 1991 but although it has been a separate country for two decades, no other nation has recognized its independence.

EGYPT

LIBYA

LIBYAN DESERT — Wadi Half

CHAD

Japal Marrah 3089 m

• El Fasher

El Obeid

• Nyala

DARFUR **SUDAN**

CENTRAL AFRICAN REPUBLIC

BAHR AL-GHAZAL

• Wau

SOUTH SUDAN

• Yambio

DEMOCRATIC REPUBLIC OF THE CONGO

Aru

Lake Albert

Lake Edward

RWANDA
Kigali

Lake Kivu

BURUNDI
Bujumbura

Kigoma •

Lake Tanganyika

0	100	200	300	400	500 mi
0	200	400	600	800 km	

*The **Maasai people** of Kenya and Tanzania wear toga-like garments called shukkas, which can be bought at roadside shops. The official colour of the Maasai tribe is red, and is always worn as clothing or jewellery.*

NUBIAN
DESERT

RED SEA

Port Sudan

Merowe
Atbara

Kassala   Keren   Massawa
Omdurman   Asmara   DAHLAK
Khartoum   ERITREA   ISLANDS

Wad Medani   Aksum   Ras Dashen
                        4533 m   Asseb
Kosti   GULF OF ADEN   Cape
       Gonder   Caseyr
Malakal   Lake   Blue Nile   DJIBOUTI
           Tana   Djibouti
Debre Markos   Blue Nile   Berbera
                        Dire Dawa
amciel   Addis Ababa   Harer   Hargeisa
                                    SOMALILAND
       Gore   Nazret
ETHIOPIA   Jima   OGADEN
                              PLATEAU   Eyl
Juba   Shebele
GANDA   GREAT RIFT VALLEY
       Mount Elgon   Lake   SOMALIA
       4322 m   Turkana
oga   KENYA   Baidoa
Kampala   Mogadishu
Kisumu   Marka
asaka   Nakuru   Nanyuki   Baraawe
Lake   Mount Kenya
ictoria   Thika   5200 m   Garissa
       Lake   Nairobi   Kismaayo
       Natron
wanza   Galana   INDIAN
       Arusha   Malindi   OCEAN
Lake
inyanga   Eyasi   Mount Kilimanjaro
                    5895 m   Mombasa
Tabora
TANZANIA   Tanga   Pemba Island
Dodoma   Zanzibar   Zanzibar Island
Rungwa   Bagamoyo
Kilosa   Dar es Salaam
Iringa   Mafia Island
Mbeya   Kilwa
Lake
Malawi   Songea   Lindi   Mtwara
IA   Ruvuma
       MOZAMBIQUE

DANAKIL VALLEY

Atbara

White Nile

Jubba

Tana

Rufiji

MALAWI

▷ **Seaweed** is farmed in coastal areas throughout Africa and Asia. It can be used as food or fertilizer and also in medicines.

In the next
...625 kg of tea will be produced in Kenya – enough for 500,000 teabags.
minute...

MOUNT KILIMANJARO [H9] is only 350 km south of the Equator, yet its summit is covered in snow and ice all year.

THE DISTANCE from the far south to the far north of Africa is 7750 km – the same as from Mexico to the North Pole.

Search and Find

Burundi	**Somalia**
• Bujumbura. . . . H7	• Mogadishu . . . F11
Djibouti	**Sudan**
• Djibouti D11	• Khartoum C8
Eritrea	**South Sudan**
• Asmara. C9	• Juba F8
Ethiopia	**Tanzania**
• Addis Ababa. . . E9	• Dar es Salaam. . I9
Kenya	• Dodoma I9
• Nairobi G9	**Uganda**
Rwanda	• Kampala G8
• Kigali G7	

Central and southern Africa

This region stretches from the tropical rainforests of Cameroon to the rich agricultural lands of **South Africa**. Only those countries with mineral wealth have prospered. Political unrest is widespread, bringing great poverty to Mozambique, the Central African Republic and Zimbabwe. Once an exporter of food and tobacco, Zimbabwe is now reliant on international aid. Farming, commerce, and gold and diamond mining have brought prosperity to many South Africans.

Victoria Falls [G8] on the Zambezi river tumbles more than 128 m into the gorge below, creating the largest sheet of falling water in the world. The local people called the waterfall 'the smoke that thunders'.

Facts and Stats

- The longest river is the Congo [C7]. At 4700 km in length, the Nile river is only 1.5 times longer.

- Mont Ngaliema (Mount Stanley) [C9] is the highest mountain at 5109 m in height – 16 times higher than the Eiffel Tower.

- The life expectancy of people in Swaziland is 49 years, compared to 75 years in Mauritius and a world average of 68 years.

Did You Know?

The Namib Desert [H6] is the oldest desert in the world. It covers 270,000 km² – more than twice the area of Iceland. Some parts have fewer than 2 cm of rain a year.

The **quiver tree** is a species of aloe found in southern Africa, especially throughout Namibia. Native people use the branches and bark of the tree to make containers, or quivers, for their arrows.

NIGERIA · Garoua
CHA
Garba
CENT
AFRICAN R
· Bouar Bambari
Mount Cameroon · Bamenda
4071 m CAMEROON Berbérati
Malabo · · Douala · Bangui
Bioko Island · Yaoundé
EQUATORIAL GUINEA
SÃO TOMÉ *Príncipe*
AND PRÍNCIPE · Libreville · Mbandak
São · · *São*
Tomé *Tomé*
Port-Gentil GABON REPUBLIC OF THE CONGO DEMOCR OF TH
Con
Lake Mai-Ndombe · Bandundu
Kasai
Brazzaville
Loubomo · · Kinshasa · Kikwit
Pointe-Noire · · Matadi
Kwilu
Tshik
Kwango
Luanda ·
Cuanza Saurimo ·
Luena
Lobito · ANGOLA ·
Benguela · · Huambo
Kwa
Namibe · · Lubango
Cubango
Cuito
Cunene
ETOSHA PAN
Cape Fria · Grootfontein ·
NAMIBIA B
Windhoek
Swakopmund · · KALAHA
Walvis Bay · DESER
· Rehoboth
NAMIB DESERT
Lüderitz · · Keetmanshoop
SO
Alexander Bay ·
Kenhardt
Carnarvon ·
Calvinia · Beaufort W
Great Karoo
Cape Town · · Worc
Cape of Good Hope Mosselb
False Bay

THE **DISTANCE** to the bottom of South Africa's deepest gold mine is 3777 m – this would take four minutes in a high-speed lift.

Search and Find

Angola	**Mauritius**
• Luanda E6	• Port Louis . . . H14
Botswana	**Mozambique**
• Gaborone H8	• Maputo I9
Cameroon	**Namibia**
• Yaoundé C5	• Windhoek H7
Central African Republic	**Republic of the Congo**
• Bangui B7	• Brazzaville . . . D6
Comoros	**São Tomé and Príncipe**
• Moroni F12	• São Tomé C4
Democratic Republic of the Congo	**Seychelles**
• Kinshasa D6	• Victoria D14
Equatorial Guinea	**South Africa**
• Malabo C5	• Cape Town J7
Gabon	• Pretoria H9
• Libreville C5	**Swaziland**
Lesotho	• Lobamba I9
• Maseru I8	• Mbabane I9
Madagascar	**Zambia**
• Antananarivo . G12	• Lusaka F9
Malawi	**Zimbabwe**
• Lilongwe F10	• Harare G9

In the next ...South Africa's diamond mines will produce enough gems for 21 pairs of earrings. minute...

0 100 200 300 400 500 mi
0 200 400 600 800 km

SEYCHELLES

Victoria

INDIAN OCEAN

Cape Delgado

COMOROS

Moroni

MAYOTTE (FRANCE)

Antsiranana

MADAGASCAR

Mahajanga

Antananarivo

MAURITIUS

RÉUNION (FRANCE)

Port Louis

Fianarantsoa

Map labels (mainland)

Bakouma
SOUTH SUDAN
Bondo
Uele
Watsa
UGANDA
Mount Ngaliema 5109 m
Basoko
Kisangani
IC REPUBLIC
Lake Edward
CONGO
Lake Kivu
RWANDA
Bukavu
BURUNDI
Lomami
Congo
Kalemie
TANZANIA
Lake Tanganyika
Mbuji-Mayi
Lake Mweru
Kamina
Lubilash
Mbala
Lake Malawi
Kasama
lwezi
Likasi
MALAWI
Lubumbashi
Lake Bangweulu
Kitwe
Mufulira
Kafue
Ndola
Lilongwe
Lúrio
Kabwe
Chipata
Nacala
ZAMBIA
Zomba
Nampula
Moçambique
Lake Cahora Bassa
Lusaka
Blantyre
Zambezi
Tete
Livingstone
Lake Kariba
Harare
Quelimane
vango
Victoria Falls
Chitungwiza
Chimoio
elta
Maun
ZIMBABWE
Beira
'WANA
Bulawayo
Save
rancistown
lebi-Phikwe
Messina
Inhambane
Molepolole
Pietersburg
Limpopo
Gaborone
MOZAMBIQUE
MOZAMBIQUE CHANNEL
atse
Pretoria
Mbabane
Maputo
Johannesburg
Soweto
Vaal
SWAZILAND
Vereeniging
Lobamba
H AFRICA
Kimberley
Maseru
emfontein
LESOTHO
Pietermaritzburg
Orange
DRAKENSBERG MOUNTAINS
Durban
delburg
Umtata
Port Shepstone
East London
Port Elizabeth

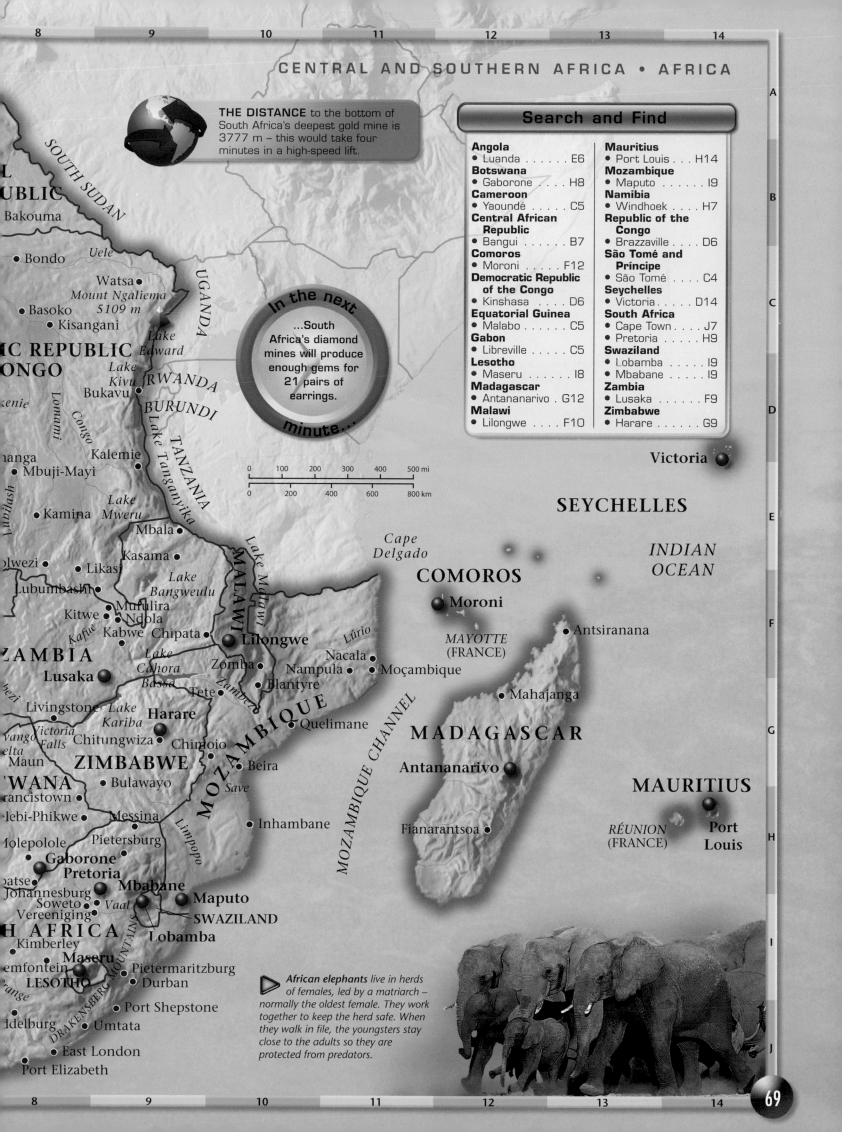

▷ **African elephants** live in herds of females, led by a matriarch – normally the oldest female. They work together to keep the herd safe. When they walk in file, the youngsters stay close to the adults so they are protected from predators.

Asia

ARCTIC OCEAN

RUSSIAN FEDERATION

KAZAKHSTAN

MONGOLIA

UZBEKISTAN

KYRGYZSTAN

TURKMENISTAN

TAJIKISTAN

TURKEY

NORTH
KOREA

CHINA

SOUTH
KOREA

JAPAN

1
SYRIA
2
IRAQ

AFGHANISTAN

3 4

5
IRAN

PAKISTAN

NEPAL

9

6
7
8

BANGLADESH

TAIWAN

SAUDI
ARABIA

BURMA
(MYANMAR)

LAOS

INDIA

*PACIFIC
OCEAN*

OMAN

THAILAND

VIETNAM

YEMEN

CAMBODIA

PHILIPPINES

SRI
LANKA

10

12

MALAYSIA

11

INDONESIA

INDIAN
OCEAN

EAST
TIMOR

KEY
1 CYPRUS
2 LEBANON
3 ISRAEL
4 JORDAN
5 KUWAIT
6 BAHRAIN
7 QATAR
8 UNITED ARAB EMIRATES
9 BHUTAN
10 BRUNEI
11 SINGAPORE
12 MALDIVES

COUNTRY FACTFILE

Country	Life expectancy	Population in thousands	Population growth %	Population as urban %	Literacy %	Area km²	Population density per km²	Capital city	Currency	Languages
Afghanistan	49	23,994	2.4	23	28	645,807	37.1	Kabul	Afghani	Dari, Pashto
Bahrain	78	1235	2.8	92	89	716	1724.9	Manama	Bahraini Dinar	Arabic, Urdu, English
Bangladesh	70	142,319	1.6	28	48	147,570	964.4	Dhaka	Taka	Bangla, English
Bhutan	68	696	1.3	36	47	46,500	15	Thimphu	Ngultrum	Dzongkha, Nepali
Brunei	76	423	1.7	76	93	5765	73.4	Bandar Seri Begawan	Bruneian Dollar	Malay
Burma (Myanmar)	65	52,171	1.1	34	90	676,577	77.1	Naypyidaw	Kyat	Burmese, Shan
Cambodia	63	13,396	1.7	22	74	181,035	74	Phnom Penh	Riel	Khmer
China	75	1,340,000	0.5	51	91	9,559,686	140.2	Beijing	Yuan	Chinese (Guoyo), Wu, Yuëh
*Cyprus	78	1121	1.6	70	98	9251	121.2	Nicosia	Euro	Greek, Turkish, English
East Timor	68	1067	2	28	59	14,874	71.7	Dili	US Dollar	Tetum, Portuguese
India	67	1,210,000	1.3	30	61	3,287,263	368.1	New Delhi	Indian Rupee	Hindi, English, Telegu, Bengali
Indonesia	72	237,641	1.1	52	90	1,904,413	124.8	Jakarta	Indonesian Rupiah	Bhasa Indonesia, Javanese, Sudanese
Iran	70	74,733	1.2	71	77	1,641,918	45.5	Tehran	Iranian Rial	Farsi (Persian), Azeri
Iraq	71	33,331	2.4	76	74	434,128	76.8	Baghdad	New Iraqi Dinar	Arabic, Kurdish
Israel	81	7695	1.6	92	98	20,400	377.2	Jerusalem	Israeli Shekel	Hebrew, Arabic
Japan	84	128,057	0.0	78	99	377,819	338.9	Tokyo	Yen	Japanese
Jordan	79	5103	2.3	79	89.9	89,342	57.1	Amman	Jordanian Dinar	Arabic
Kazakhstan	70	16,675	0.4	59	99	2,717,300	6.1	Astana	Tenge	Kazakh, Russian
Korea, North	69	24,052	0.4	61	99	122,762	195.9	Pyongyang	North Korean Won	Korean
Korea, South	79	48,219	0.2	83	98	99,461	484.6	Seoul	South Korean Won	Korean
Kuwait	77	2496	2	98	93	17,818	140	Kuwait City	Kuwaiti Dinar	Arabic, Farsi, English
Kyrgyzstan	69	5418	1.4	35	99	198,500	27.1	Bishkek	Som	Kyrgyz, Russian
Laos	53	6128	1.7	33	73	236,800	25.9	Vientiane	Kip	Lao
Lebanon	75	4220	0.2	90	87	10,201	413.7	Beirut	Lebanese Pound	Arabic
Malaysia	74	28,334	1.6	72	89	329,847	85.9	Kuala Lumpur, Putrajaya	Ringgit	Bahasa Melayu (Malay), Chinese, English
Maldives	75	315	0.0	40	94	298	1057	Male	Rufiyaa	Dhivehi (Maldivian)
Mongolia	69	2648	1.5	62	98	1,564,100	1.7	Ulaanbaatar	Tugrik	Khalkha Mongol
Nepal	67	26,621	1.6	19	49	147,181	180.9	Kathmandu	Nepalese Rupee	Nepali, Maithali
Oman	74	2773	2	81	81	309,500	9	Muscat	Omani Rial	Arabic, Baluchi
Pakistan	66	192,289	1.6	38	50	796,095	241.5	Islamabad	Pakistani Rupee	Urdu, Punjabi, Sindhi
Philippines	72	92,338	1.9	65	93	300,076	307.7	Manila	Philippine Peso	Filipino (Tagalog), Cebuano, English
Qatar	78	1699	1	96	89	11,427	148.7	Doha	Qatari Rial	Arabic, Hindi, Malayalam
Russian Federation	66	142,905	-0.5	78	99	17,075,400	8.4	Moscow	Rouble	Russian, Tatar, Ukrainian
Saudi Arabia	74	27,137	1.5	86	79	2,149,690	12.6	Riyadh	Saudi Riyal	Arabic, Malayalam, Tagalog
Singapore	84	5077	0.8	100	95	697	7212.6	Singapore	Singapore Dollar	Chinese, Malay, English
Sri Lanka	76	20,653	0.9	23	91	65,610	314.8	Colombo, Kotte	Sri Lankan Rupee	Sinhala, Tamil
Syria	75	21,377	2.9	56	80	185,180	115.4	Damascus	Syrian Pound	Arabic
Taiwan	78	23,225	0.2	75	97	36,179	641.9	Taipei	Taiwan dollar	Chinese (Mandarin), Min
Tajikistan	66	7374	1.8	28	98	143,100	51.5	Dushanbe	Somoni	Tajik, Uzbek
Thailand	74	65,479	0.6	35	93	514,000	130.6	Bangkok	Baht	Thai, Chinese
Turkey	73	74,724	1.2	75	88	780,580	95.9	Ankara	Turkish Lira	Turkish, Kurdish
Turkmenistan	69	6550	1.1	50	99	488,100	11.6	Ashgabat	Turkmen Manat	Turkmen, Uzbek
United Arab Emirates	77	7500	3.3	90	78	83,600	89.7	Abu Dhabi	Emirati Dirham	Arabic, Hindu, Urdu
Uzbekistan	73	29,123	0.9	39	99.	444,103	65.6	Tashkent	Uzbek Soum	Uzbek, Russian
Vietnam	72	85,847	1.1	30	90	329,315	260.7	Hanoi	Dong	Vietnamese
Yemen	64	22,492	2.6	32	50	527,970	42.6	Sanaa	Yemeni Rial	Arabic

*NB: Cyprus is part of Europe, but the mapping can be found in the Asia section.

The Near East

A poor, mountainous region, Turkey has a beautiful coastline and thriving tourist industry. The country is currently being transformed by the Great Anatolian project – reservoirs will be built along the Tigris and Euphrates rivers, to irrigate 16,000 km² of land. Although geographically closer to Asia, Turkey is internationally recognized as part of Europe. Israel was created in 1948. Land was taken from the Palestinians resulting in conflict with Syria, Jordan and Lebanon. Sheep and goats are the main livestock. Where irrigation is possible, vegetables and fruit are grown, much of which is exported to Europe.

BULGARIA

GREECE

• Edirne

Bosporus Strait

Tekirdag• • Istanbul

Sea of Marmara

• Izmit

• Bursa *Sakary*

Balikesir • Eskisehir•

• Kütahya

A N A T O

P L A T

• Manisa Usak•

• Izmir

Ephesus• Nazilli

Aydin • • Denizli

• Ispar

• Bodrum

T A

Antalya •

▷ The **Temple Mount** in Jerusalem [I9] is an important religious site. The Dome of the Rock is a Muslim shrine. The Western Wall dates back to 500 BC and is used by Jews for prayer.

THE DISTANCE from Europe to Asia across the Bosporus Strait [B6] is only 700 m and takes one minute by car across a bridge.

Search and Find

Cyprus
• Nicosia F8

Israel
• Jerusalem I9

Jordan
• Amman H10

Lebanon
• Beirut G9

Syria
• Damascus . . . H10

Turkey
• Ankara C8

Did You Know?

Cyprus is the third largest island in the Mediterranean. The northern area of the island is Turkish Cypriot and the southern area is Greek Cypriot. Although geographically closer to Asia, Cyprus joined the EU in 2004.

Facts and Stats

• Turkey's area of 780,580 km² is 7.5 times the area of Iceland.

• Mount Ararat [D14] is the highest mountain at 5137 m –16 times higher than the Eiffel Tower.

• The life expectancy of people in Israel is 81 years, compared to 75 years in Syria and a world average of 68 years.

▷ *Pamukkale*, which means 'cotton castle' in Turkish, was formed from the water of a very hot spring. The water contains a lot of chalk, which results in the limestone cliffs that can be seen today.

8 9 10 11 12 13 14

0   50   100   150   200 mi
0   100   200   300 km

The **Dead Sea** [I9] is the second saltiest body of water in the world and is called 'dead' because fish and other organisms cannot survive in it. Salty deposits cover the beaches and cliffs, and it is almost impossible to sink in the water because of the high salt content.

BLACK SEA

GEORGIA
ARMENIA

Zonguldak
Karabük
Samsun
Ordu   Trabzon
Çorum
PONTIC MOUNTAINS
Kars
Kelkit
Erzurum
Ankara
Kirikkale
Sivas
Erzincan
Mount Ararat 5137 m
TURKEY
Malatya
Elazig
Murat
Lake Van   Van
Kizilirmak
Kayseri
Lake Tuz
Adiyaman
Diyarbakir
Batman
IRAN
Konya
Firat
US MOUNTAINS
Tarsus   Adana
Osmaniye   Gaziantep
Khabur
Al Qamishli
Mersin
Al Hasakah
Antakya
Al Bab
Aleppo
Ar Raqqah
Euphrates

CYPRUS
Latakia
Lake Assad
Dayr az Zawr
Paphos   Nicosia
Baniyas
Hamah
SYRIA
Limassol
Tartus
Hims
LEBANON MOUNTAINS
Tripoli
Abu Kamal
LEBANON
SYRIAN DESERT
Beirut
MEDITERRANEAN SEA
Sidon
IRAQ
Tyre
Damascus
GOLAN HEIGHTS
Al Kiswah
Acre
Al Qunaytirah
Haifa
Sea of Galilee
Nazareth
Dar'a
Hadera
WEST BANK
Irbid
Netanya
Jordan
Az-Zarqa
Ramallah
Amman
Tel Aviv
Jerusalem   Dead Sea
Gaza   Bethlehem
Ma'daba
GAZA STRIP
Beersheba
Al-Karak
ISRAEL
Wadi al Hasa
EGYPT
NEGEV DESERT   Ma'an
JORDAN
Elat   Aqaba
SAUDI ARABIA
Gulf of Aqaba

In the next ...Turkey will produce enough Turkish delight confectionery to create a pillar 305 m in height. minute...

The ruins of Ephesus [D5] are a major tourist attraction. Built in 135 AD, the restored **Library of Celsus** is a monumental tomb for Celsus Polemaeanus, the governor of Asia. His grave is across the entrance, under the ground floor.

A B C D E F G H I J

The Middle East

Vast oil and gas reserves have made several countries in the Middle East some of the wealthiest in the world. However, before oil was discovered, this was a poor region of desert tribes and coastal fishing. The area between the Euphrates and Tigris rivers was once home to the great civilization of Mesopotamia. Recent wars have damaged the economies of Iran and Iraq, but other countries such as Bahrain are investing in tourism and other forms of industry. The city of Dubai now has the largest indoor ski slope in the world.

*For thousands of years, Iran has been the centre of the hand-woven **Persian carpet** industry. Although machinery is widely used today, traditional methods are still used in some areas. A medium-sized rug can take a skilled worker up to a year to complete.*

Extreme Weather

Midday temperatures can reach 50°C in the desert areas, but snow is common in the mountains of Iran and Iraq.

Did You Know?

The United Arab Emirates obtains more than 80 percent of its water supply by desalinating sea water.

*Millions of Muslims have made a pilgrimage, or Hajj, to Mecca [G5]. The holiest place in Islam is the **Kaaba**. Non-Muslims cannot enter Mecca.*

ARMENIA

TURKEY

Tab

SYRIA

Mosul • Arbil

Kirkuk •

I R A Q

Bakhtar

Baghdad ●

S Y R I A N

Tigris

D E S E R T

Karbala •

Euphrates

Najaf •

JORDAN

An Nasiriyah •

EGYPT

Al Jawf • • Sakakah

N A F U D

D E S E R T

H I J A Z

Buraydah •

Shaqra •

• Medina

Riyadh

• Yanbu

S A U D

RED SEA

Jiddah •

• Mecca

• Taif

As-Sulayyil •

A S I R

• Abha

• Jizan

• Harad

● **Sanaa**

• Al-Hudaydah

GU

• Ta'izz

Shaq

Aden •

GU

TURKMENISTAN

CASPIAN SEA

Rasht

Babol
Gorgan

ELBURZ MOUNTAINS
Karaj
Tehran

Mashhad

AFGHANISTAN

Qom

Hamadan

Kashan

IRAN

Esfahan

Yazd

ZAGROS MOUNTAINS

Ahvaz

Kerman

Zahedan

Basra
Abadan

PAKISTAN

Shiraz

KUWAIT
Kuwait
City

Bushehr

PERSIAN GULF

Bandar-e
Lengeh
Bandar 'Abbas

Strait of Hormuz

Jask

Al Qatif
BAHRAIN
l-Dammam
Manama
QATAR

Sharjah
Dubai

Suhar

GULF OF OMAN

Al-Hufuf
Doha

Abu Dhabi

Jabal ash Sham
3035 m
Matrah
Muscat

UNITED ARAB
EMIRATES

Nizwa
Sur

ARABIAN SEA

RABIA

Khaluf

EMPTY QUARTER

OMAN

Salalah

YEMEN

Al Mukalla

SOCOTRA
(YEMEN)

ADEN

Search and Find

Bahrain	**Qatar**
• Manama E8	• Doha F9
Iran	**Saudi Arabia**
• Tehran B9	• Riyadh F7
Iraq	**United Arab**
• Baghdad . . . C7	**Emirates**
Kuwait	• Abu Dhabi . . . F10
• Kuwait City . . . D8	**Yemen**
Oman	• Sanaa I7
• Muscat F11	

THE DISTANCE from Yemen to Africa is only 30 km across the Red Sea and takes four hours by canoe.

Facts and Stats

• The average income per person in Qatar is £45,600, compared to a world average of £5640.

• Saudi Arabia has an area of 2.2 million km² and is 21 times the area of Iceland.

• The longest river is the Euphrates [C7]. At 2800 km in length, it is nearly 2.5 times shorter than the Nile river.

In the next
...Saudi Arabia will produce 850,000 litres of oil – enough for a car to travel 10 million km.
minute...

0	100	200	300	400 mi
0	200	400	600 km	

*Built in the 1970s, **Kuwait's water towers** [D8] are more than 145 m in height. One tower provides electricity, and the other two towers store water – the middle tower holds more than 4 million litres of water. The main tower also has a viewing platform and revolving restaurant.*

Indian subcontinent

With ice-covered mountains, tropical lowlands and hot deserts, this region is one of contrasts. Afghanistan is a war-torn, semi-desert nation that is in the process of rebuilding amidst ongoing conflicts. India has one of the most rapidly growing economies in the world. A highly educated, English-speaking workforce has resulted in many European and American companies establishing various support operations in India. The 'Bollywood' film studios are a worldwide success and cities are rapidly expanding. However, out of India's 1.1 billion population, two-thirds remain poor, rural farmers. Pakistan, Bangladesh and the Himalayan states of Nepal and Bhutan remain relatively undeveloped.

The **Taj Mahal** in Agra [D9], India, was built for Mumtaz Mahal, the wife of Emperor Shah Jahan. When she died in 1629, the Emperor ordered the most beautiful tomb in the world to be built. It took 20,000 workers about 20 years to build. The Emperor and his wife are buried beneath the 60-m-high white dome.

Search and Find

Afghanistan
- Kabul B7

Bangladesh
- Dhaka E11

Bhutan
- Thimphu D11

India
- New Delhi D9

Nepal
- Kathmandu . . D10

Pakistan
- Islamabad B8

Sri Lanka
- Colombo J9
- Kotte J9

Did You Know?

Great Britain ruled India until 1947. This is why English is widely spoken and cricket is the national sport.

THE DISTANCE from the Everest base camp to the summit is 10 km. In 2000, it was climbed in less than 17 hours.

World Record

In 1985, Mawsynram [E12] recorded the world's highest yearly rainfall – over 26,000 mm.

Many Hindus go to a 'mandir', or **temple**, to say prayers and to make offerings of food to the gods. The temples are beautifully decorated with carvings of gods and spirits.

Map labels

TURKMENISTAN
Sheberghan
Mazar-e Shar
Herat
AFGHANISTA
IRAN
Farah
Kabu
Helmand
Qandahar
RIGESTAN DESERT
Quetta
PAKISTA
SUL
Larkana
Sukk
Gwadar
Indus
Hyderabad
Karachi
Mirpur Kh
Gulf of Kachchh
RANN OF KACHCHH
Ahmadaba
Jamnagar
ARABIAN SEA
Bhavnagar
Sur
Gulf of Khambhat
Mumbai (Bombay)
INDIAN OCEAN

SIGIRIYA, or Lion's Mouth, was the fortress of Sri Lankan King Kashyapa (AD 477–495). Only the two giant paws of the lion remain.

Facts and Stats

- The longest river in the region is the Brahmaputra [D12]. At 2900 km in length, it is almost half the length of the Nile river.

- The highest mountain in the world is Mount Everest [D11] at 8848 m in height – 28 times higher than the Eiffel Tower.

- The life expectancy of people in Afghanistan is 49 years, compared to 76 years in Sri Lanka and a world average of 68 years.

Extreme Weather

The heaviest recorded hailstones, weighing up to one kg killed 92 people in Bangladesh on 14 April 1986.

TAJIKISTAN

K2
8611 m

Mardan
Islamabad
shawar
awalpindi
Srinagar
isalabad • Gujranwala
Lahore • Amritsar
ultan • Sahiwal
Sutlej • Ludhiana
hawalpur • Chandigarh

CHINA

HIMALAYAS

Meerut
Delhi
New Delhi
Jaipur • Agra
odhpur • Ajmer
Ganges
Yamuna
Udaipur
Lalitpur

Bhopal
dodara
Narmada
Indore
INDIA

NEPAL
Kathmandu
Mount Everest
8848 m
Lucknow
Kanpur
Varanasi
Allahabad
Patna
Biratnagar
Rangpur
Rajshahi
Dhanbad
Jamshedpur
Khulna
Kolkata
(Calcutta)

Thimphu
BHUTAN
Brahmaputra
Jorhat
Guwahati
NAGA HILLS
Mawsynram
Sylhet • Imphal
BANGLADESH
Dhaka • Agartala
Chittagong

BURMA (MYANMAR)

Nagpur • Raipur
Godavari
EASTERN GHATS
Cuttack

BAY OF BENGAL

une
ona)
Solapur
Hyderabad
Krishna
olhapur
Kurnool
ubli-Dhawar
Vishakhapatnam
Vijayawada

The **Ganges river** flows through the city of Varanasi [E10] and is believed to be sacred. Many Hindus make pilgrimages to pray and bathe in the holy water.

Nellore
Bengaluru
(Bangalore)
ngalore
Chennai
(Madras)
Mysore
Puducherry
Kozhikode (Calicut)
Coimbatore
Tiruchchirappalli

ANDAMAN
ISLANDS
(INDIA)

Kochi
Cochin)
Madurai
Palk Strait
Jaffna
hiruvananthapuram
rivandrum)
Trincomalee

SRI LANKA
Colombo
Kandy
Kotte
Galle

NICOBAR
ISLANDS
(INDIA)

| 0 | 100 | 200 | 300 | 400 mi |
| 0 | 200 | 400 | 600 km |

...more than 50 babies will be born in India – that's 66,000 every day.

In the next minute...

Vietnam and the Philippines

Lush tropical rainforests lead to wonderful sandy beaches and warm seas. Rice fields and remote villages give way to sprawling cities. Despite the rapid growth of tourism in Thailand and Vietnam, most of this area is poor. Many people live near the coast and they are still mainly dependent on fishing and farming. Rice is the main crop, grown in the river valleys in wet paddy fields. Wars in Vietnam and Cambodia have devastated many cities, leaving Cambodia with the highest number of widows and orphans in the world.

	0	100	200	300	400 mi
0	200	400	600 km		

CHINA

Thai Nguyen

Hanoi ● ● Haiphong
Nam Dinh ●

Thanh Hoa ● *Gulf of Tonkin*

BURMA (MYANMAR)

Mandalay ●

Luang Prabang ●

Vinh ●

Sittwe ●

Naypyidaw ●

Irrawaddy

LAOS

Chiang Mai ●

Vientiane ●

Hué ●

Prome ●

Udon Thani ●

Savannakhet ● Da Nang ●

THAILAND

Henzada ●

Khon Kaen ●

Pakxe ●

Bassein ●

Pegu ● Yangon (Rangoon) ●

Ubon Ratchathani ●

Champassak ●

Moulmein ●

Nakhon Sawan ●

Gulf of Martaban

Qui Nhon ●

Tavoy ●

Nakhon Ratchasima ●

Angkor Wat ◆

VIETNAM

ANDAMAN SEA

Bangkok ●

Batdâmbang ●

Nha Trang ●

Chon Buri ●

CAMBODIA

Da Lat ●

Mergui ●

Kampong Cham ●

Phnom Penh ●

Ho Chi Minh City ●

GULF OF THAILAND

Can Tho ●

Mekong

Facts and Stats

• The life expectancy of people in Cambodia is 63 years, compared to 74 years in Thailand and a world average of 68 years.

• The largest city in the region is Bangkok, with 13.2 million inhabitants.

• The average income per person in Cambodia is £495, compared to a world average of £5640.

SPRATLY ISLANDS

In the next ...the Mekong river [G5] will deposit enough silt to fill 50 bathtubs – 30 million tonnes a year. **minute...**

Nakhon Si Thammarat

Phuket ●

Hat Yai ● ● Songkhla

MALAYSIA

▷ Many young men in Thailand temporarily become **Buddhist monks** to learn more about their faith. They shave their heads and beards and wear robes to show commitment to the holy life.

Search and Find

Cambodia		**Philippines**	
• Phnom Penh	. . H5	• Manila	. . . . . F10
Laos		**Thailand**	
• Vientiane	. . . . . F4	• Bangkok	. . . . . H4
Burma (Myanmar)		**Vietnam**	
• Naypyidaw	. . . . F2	• Hanoi	. . . . E5

THE DISTANCE from Yangon [G2] to Bangkok [H4] is 640 km and would take an elephant three days of non-stop walking.

▷ The canals in Bangkok [H4] are used for **floating markets** where fresh produce, such as fruit, vegetables and flowers, is sold from boats.

Luzon Strait

BABUYAN ISLANDS

Laoag •

• Tuguegarao

Luzon

PHILIPPINES

PACIFIC OCEAN

• Cabanatuan

Angeles •

• Quezon City

Manila ◉

Batangas •

Mindoro

• Calbayog
Samar

SOUTH CHINA SEA

• Ormoc
Leyte

Panay Bacolod •

Iloilo • • Cebu

Negros

Butuan •

Cagayan de Oro •

Mindanao

• Puerto Princesa

Palawan

Pagadian •

Davao •

SULU SEA

General Santos •

Moro Gulf

Zamboanga •

CELEBES SEA

Balabac Strait

Did You Know?

The ruins of the ancient city of Angkor Wat [G5], complete with Hindu temples and royal palaces, were discovered in the Cambodian rainforest 150 years ago.

Extreme Weather

In July, the monsoon rains bring the city of Yangon [G2] as much rain as London gets in a year.

SULU ARCHIPELAGO

▷ Many tropical countries suffer from rainy seasons called monsoons, which result in serious flooding. In some parts of Asia, **houses are built on stilts** over bodies of water to protect them against water damage.

Indonesia, Malaysia and Singapore

Situated on the Equator, this region has a hot, wet climate. Malaysia is part of the Asian mainland and the large island of Borneo. It is developing rapidly with car and shipbuilding industries. Singapore is the richest country in this region, based on its technology industry, banking and high educational standards. A safe, law-abiding nation, laws against all types of crime, even dropping litter, are strictly enforced. Indonesia consists of over 13,000 islands. Natural disasters, poor communications and corruption have restricted economic growth. Although East Timor became independent from Indonesia in 2002, it remains impoverished.

THAILAND

George Town
Kuala Terengganu
Ipoh
MALAY
PENINSULA
Medan
Kelang
Kuala Lumpur
Putrajaya
MALAYSIA
Johor Baharu
Singapore
SINGAPORE
Pekanbaru
Sumatra
Padang
Bangka
Jambi
Belitung
Palembang

Kota Kinabalu
Sandakan
Bandar Seri Begawan
BRUNEI
SABAH
Natuna Island
CELEBES SEA
SARAWAK
Kuching
Manado
Pontianak
Kapuas
MOLUCCAS SEA
KALIMANTAN
Makassar Strait
Palu
Balikpapan
Sulawesi
Borneo
Barito
Banjarmasin

INDONESIA

Tanjungkarang
Telukbetung
Jakarta
JAVA SEA
Makasar
Bandung
Java
Semarang
FLORES SEA
Surakarta
Surabaya
Malang
Komodo
Flores
Bali
Mataram
Ende
Lombok
Sumbawa
Sumba
Kupang
Tim[...]

◁ More than 450 m in height, the **Petronas Towers** in Kuala Lumpur [E2] contain 88 floors of offices, a shopping mall, a concert hall and parking for 4500 cars.

Extreme Weather

At the Equator, the climate is the same throughout the year – hot and very wet. Singapore's temperature averages at 27°C.

...five new cars will be made in this region – that's 2.6 million a year.

▷ **Tea** has been grown throughout Indonesia for more than 200 years, especially in Java and Sumatra. These small islands now produce 7 percent of the world's tea exports. The shoots are picked by hand, packed and exported.

C

Did You Know?

The 2004 tsunami in southeast Asia was caused by an undersea earthquake. The waves travelled at speeds of up to 800 km/h – 230,000 people were killed and five million were made homeless.

Search and Find

Brunei
• Bandar Seri Begawan E5
East Timor
• Dili H7
Indonesia
• Jakarta H3

Malaysia
• Kuala Lumpur . . E2
• Putrajaya E2
Singapore
• Singapore F2

D

THE DISTANCE from Singapore to Malaysia is only 1056 m and the Joho–Singapore Causeway can be crossed by car in one minute.

E

| 0 | 100 | 200 | 300 | 400 mi |

| 0 | 200 | 400 | 600 km |

Malmahera

F

Sorong

Jayapura •

SERAM SEA

Seram

Ambon ○

New Guinea

G

u

NDA SEA

ARU ISLANDS

ar

Tanimbar Island

ARAFURA SEA

H

cau

ST TIMOR

▷ The **Batak people** live in Sumatra, Indonesia. Easily recognizable, their houses are built on stilts and have high, thatched roofs. Often ornaments and paintings are placed on the outside to ward away evil spirits.

Facts and Stats

• The average income per person in Singapore is £26,740 compared to £310 in East Timor and a world average of £5640.

• The life expectancy of people in Singapore is 84 years, compared to 74 years in Malaysia and a world average of 68 years.

• Indonesia's area of 1.9 million km² is 18 times the area of Iceland.

I

J

Japan

Japan consists of four main islands – Kyushu, Hokkaido, Honshu and Shikoku. More than 70 percent of the country is covered with forested volcanic mountains such as Mount Fuji. Most of Japan's population lives on the flatlands along the coast, resulting in a very high population density. People live in high-rise flats or small houses, but frequent earthquakes can cause immense damage. Agriculture, industry, and urban development are concentrated on the main island of Honshu in the area between Osaka and Tokyo. Japan is one of the richest nations in the world, with well-known brands such as Toyota, Honda, Nissan, Sony, Panasonic and JVC.

The Golden Pavilion, Kyoto [G8], was originally built in the 14th century for a samurai general. The temple has been destroyed many times, and was most recently rebuilt in the 1950s. The pavilion, except the basement floor, is covered in pure gold leaf.

World Record

The Seikan tunnel is the longest railway in the world at 54 km in length.

SEA OF JAPAN

MOUNT FUJI [G9] is an active volcano, but last erupted in 1707. More than 200,000 people walk to its snow-capped summit each year.

0	50	100	150	200 mi
0	100	200	300 km	

THE DISTANCE from Tokyo [G10] to Osaka [H8] is 515 km. It only takes 2.5 hours by high-speed train, travelling at 206 km/h.

Sumo wrestling is a popular sport in Japan. Competitors have a body weight of up to 270 kg and their aim is to push their opponent out of the ring. Sumo is more than 2000 years old, and has strict rules and ceremonies.

Oki Island

Matsue • • Yonago • Totto
Korea Strait

Tsushima

Hiroshima • Okayama • Ko
Shimonoseki • Kure • Takamatsu •
Kitakyushu • Hofu Wakaya
Fukuoka • Matsuyama Tokushima
Bungo Channel • Kochi
Sasebo • Oita • *Shikoku*
Kumamoto • Saiki •
Nagasaki •
Amakusa Island Nobeoka •
Kyushu
Koshiki Island
Miyazaki •
Miyakonojo
Kagoshima

Tanega Island
Yaku Island

Soya Strait

Rebun Island • Wakkanai

Rishiri Island

• Abashiri

Ishikari • Asahikawa
Hokkaido

Otaru • • Ebetsu • Kushiro
Sapporo • Chitose • Obihiro
Tomakomai

• Muroran

Uchiura Bay

Hakodate •   Cape
                     Erimo

Tsugaru Strait

Aomori •
Hirosaki • • Hachinohe

Akita •   • Miyako
Hanamaki •   • Kamaishi

Sakata •   • Kesennuma

Yamagata •   • Ishinomaki
             • Sendai
Sado
Island • Niigata
                • Fukushima
Nagaoka • Aizu • Koriyama

Honshu
                    • Iwaki
Toyama •
Shinano Utsunomiya • • Hitachi
     • Nagano
nazawa •   • Takasaki • Mito
• Komatsu Matsumoto • Saitama
kui Kofu • Tokyo
JAPAN   PACIFIC
   Mount Fuji   OCEAN
Gifu • 3776 m   • Chiba
yoto   • Kawasaki
Nagoya • Toyota • Fuji Yokohama
aka • Toyohashi Shizuoka
kai • Hamamatsu

              Miyake
              Island

              Hachijo
              Island

> **Geisha** are female Japanese entertainers who are skilled in many traditional arts, such as music, singing and dancing. Although the make-up and clothing of geisha change throughout their career, they generally wear a white base, red lipstick and black outlines to their eyes.

In the next

...Japan will manufacture 15 cars and 50 computer consoles.

minute...

Did You Know?

People in Japan often wear face masks to protect themselves from fumes, pollution and germs.

Extreme Weather

The mountains of the northern island of Hokkaido have some of the heaviest snowfall in the world. The 1972 Winter Olympics were held there.

◁ With so many people, cars and businesses crammed into a small area, **Tokyo** [G10] is one of the most congested cities in the world. Tokyo Tower is based on the Eiffel Tower, Paris, although it is actually more than 8 m taller.

Facts and Stats

• The highest mountain is Mount Fuji [G9] at 3776 m. It is 12 times higher than the Eiffel Tower.

• The life expectancy of people in Japan is 84 years, compared to a world average of 68 years.

• The average income per person in Japan is £26,430, compared to a world average of £5640.

China and Korea

One-fifth of the world's population lives in China, despite each family being limited to just one child. Once a poor, rural nation, China has the fastest-growing economy in the world. Each year, millions of farm workers move to the cities to work in factories. A new power station has to be built every week, making China the biggest user of coal and oil in the world. In contrast, Mongolia has a small, mainly rural population. North Korea is a Communist state with a low standard of living, but South Korea is much richer due to its shipbuilding, electronic and car industries.

In 210–209 BC, thousands of **terracotta soldiers** were buried with the first emperor of China, Qin Shi Huangdi, as it was believed to make him powerful in heaven. The tomb was discovered in 1974 near Xi'an [F10].

Search and Find

China	South Korea
• Beijing E11	• Seoul E13
Mongolia	**Taiwan**
• Ulaanbaatar . . . C9	• Taipei H13
North Korea	
• Pyongyang . . . D12	

LHASA [H7] in the Himalayas is the capital of Tibet and home to many Buddhist monasteries and ancient palaces.

THE DISTANCE from one end of The Great Wall of China to the other is 3460 km – nearly half the length of the Nile river.

Facts and Stats

• China has a population of 1340 million, which would fill 13,400 Olympic stadiums. Mongolia's population of 2.6 million would only fill 26 stadiums.

• China's area of 9.6 million km² is 93 times the area of Iceland.

• The Chang Jiang (Yangtze) [G10] is the longest river at 6300 km in length. The Nile river is nearly twice as long.

One of China's largest cities, **Shanghai** [F12] has a population of 14.2 million. The skyline is dominated by high-rise office buildings and the city is rapidly becoming one of the most important financial centres in the world. The Oriental Pearl Tower is the fifth highest tower in the world at 468 m.

Map labels

Ulaangor
ALTAI MOUNTAIN
Uliastay
KAZAKHSTAN
Tacheng
Yining
Urumqi
Turpan
Bosten Hu
KYRGYZSTAN
Korla
TARIM BASIN
TAJIKISTAN
Kashi
SINKIANG
AFGHANISTAN
Shache
TAKLIMAKAN DESERT
ALTUN SHAN
Hotan
Golmud
PAKISTAN
KUNLUN SHAN
TIBET
Amdo
INDIA
Gar
PLATEAU O
HIMALAYAS
NEPAL
Lhasa
Gyangzê
Mount Everest 8850 m
INI
BHUTAN

84

8   9   10   11   12   13   14

A

B

In the next
...China will generate enough electricity to make a cup of coffee for every person in the world.
minute...

• Gulian

• Heihe

RUSSIAN FEDERATION

• Nenjiang

• Hailar

• Qiqihar

Sühbaatar •

• Harbin

C

Hatgal • Darhan •   Choybalsan •

• Erdenet   Tamsagbulag

• Jilin

• Jargalan

Changchun •

• Chongjin

Ulaanbaatar ●

Hyesan •   **NORTH KOREA**

Fushun •

Shenyang •   Hamhung •

MONGOLIA   Saynshand •

Anshan •

SEA OF JAPAN

D

GOBI DESERT   *INNER MONGOLIA*

Jinzhou •   Sinuiju •   • Wonsan

Dalandzadgad •

Nampo •   ● **Pyongyang**

Sariwon •   **SOUTH**

Hohhot •   Zhangjiakou •   ● **Beijing**   Dalian •   **Seoul** ●   **KOREA**

Baotou •   • Tianjin   Inchon •   Taegu •

• Yantai   Taejon •   Pusan •

• Yumen   Kwangju •   *Korea Strait*

LIAN SHAN   Taiyuan •   • Zibo

Yinchuan •   • Jinan   • Qingdao   *YELLOW SEA*

E

Qinghai Hu   **CHINA**   *Huang*

• Xining   Zhengzhou •   Xuzhou •   • Lianyungang

• Lanzhou   • Luoyang

PACIFIC OCEAN

F

• Xi'an

Nanjing •

Hefei •   • Shanghai

Hangzhou •   • Ningbo

Wuhan •

Chang Jiang (Yangtze)   *Poyang Hu*

TIBET   Chengdu •   • Nanchong   *Dongting Hu*   Wenzhou •

Chongqing •   Changsha •   • Nanchang

EAST CHINA SEA

G

• Qamdo

Nu Jiang

Fuzhou •   ● **Taipei**

Hengyang •   *Taiwan Strait*

H

Guiyang •   Xiamen •   **TAIWAN**

MYANMAR

Kunming •   Liuzhou •

Guangzhou •   • Shenzen

• Hong Kong

Mekong   • Nanning   Macau •

I

LAOS   *VIETNAM*   • Zhanjiang

SOUTH CHINA SEA

• Haikou

Gulf of Tonkin   *Hainan*

Did You Know?

More than 600 years ago, the Chinese began to bake pottery at temperatures high enough to produce porcelain. When this pottery came to Europe, it was called 'china'.

J

0   100   200   300   400 mi

0   200   400   600 km

8   9   10   11   12   13   14

East Russia

The Russian Federation is the largest country in the world. However, eastern Russia contains large areas that are unpopulated. Vast areas north of the Arctic Circle suffer freezing conditions that make farming impossible. To the south, much is covered by forest or grassland. Towns are found only where there are natural resources, such as coal, oil, gas, iron and uranium. Kazakhstan is rapidly becoming wealthy due to selling oil, gas and metals to Europe and China, but Turkmenistan, Uzbekistan, Tajikistan and Kyrgyzstan remain underdeveloped.

Extreme Weather

In January 1926, Oymyakon [F10] recorded the lowest temperature for any permanently inhabited location on Earth at –71.2°C.

In the next ...11,000 Russians will be playing chess, making it the nation's most popular sport. *minute...*

SEVERNAYA ZEMLYA

ARCTIC OCEAN

KARA SEA

SIBERIA

RUSSIAN

- Vorkuta
- Noril'sk

Yenisey

Tunguska

- Serov
- Surgut
- Nizhnevartovsk

Ob

Angara

Lena

- Yekaterinburg
- Kurgan
- Chelyabinsk
- Omsk
- Tomsk
- Krasnoyarsk
- Kansk
- Ust'Ilimsk
- Kemerovo
- Novosibirsk
- Bratsk
- Semey
- Kokshetau
- Novokuznetsk
- Abakan
- Usol'ye-Sibirskoye
- Barnaul
- Pavlodar
- Angarsk
- Irkutsk
- Chita
- Ulan-Ud

YABL MOU

Lake Baikal

- Orenburg

Astana

- Aqtobe
- Oskemen

MONGOLIA

- Qaraghandy

Ural

- Atyrau
- Zhezkazgan

Lake Balkhash

KAZAKHSTAN

Ustyurt Plateau

Aral Sea

- Qyzylorda
- Taldyqorgan

CHINA

- Aktau **UZBEKISTAN**
- Almaty

CASPIAN SEA

Tashkent • **Bishkek**

KYRGYZSTAN

TURKMENISTAN

- Samarkand
- Balkanabat

Amu-Darya

Dushanbe

Ashgabat

TAJIKISTAN

IRAN

AFGHANISTAN *PAKISTAN*

Search and Find

Lake Baikal [H7] is the oldest and deepest lake in the world at 1637 m in depth. It holds more than 20 percent of the world's fresh water.

Facts and Stats

- Turkmenistan's population of 6.6 million would fill 66 stadiums.
- The life expectancy in Russia is 66 years, compared to a world average of 68 years.
- The average income per person in Russia is £6490, compared to £495 in Tajikistan and a world average of £5640.

THE DISTANCE from Moscow in European Russia to the far east of Russia takes six days and four hours to travel by train at 62 km/h.

Did You Know?

Russia has 9 time zones. When it is 12 p.m. in Moscow, it is 3 p.m. in Novosibirsk [H5] and 7 p.m. in Vladivostok [I9].

LAPTEV SEA

EAST SIBERIAN SEA

CHUKCHI SEA

Lena

VERKHOYANSKIY MOUNTAINS

CHERSKIY MOUNTAINS

Kolyma

Yakutsk•

Oymyakon•

BERING SEA

•EDERATION

Magadan•

0	250	500	750	1000 mi
0	400	800	1200	1600 km

SEA OF OKHOTSK

OV Y Y
A I N S

Amur

Petropavlovsk-Kamchatskiy•

VLADIVOSTOK [I9] is home to the Russian navy's Pacific fleet. Until 1991, foreigners were not allowed into the city in case they were spies.

CHINA

Blagoveshchensk•

•Komsomol'sk-na-Amure

Khabarovsk•

PACIFIC OCEAN

SIKHOTE-ALIN MOUNTAINS

•Yuzhno-Sakhalinsk

Vladivostok•

NORTH KOREA

The Aral Sea [I3] has shrunk by 90 percent since 1960. The remaining water has become very salty, killing off so many fish that the commercial fishing industry stopped and many boats have been abandoned.

Oceania

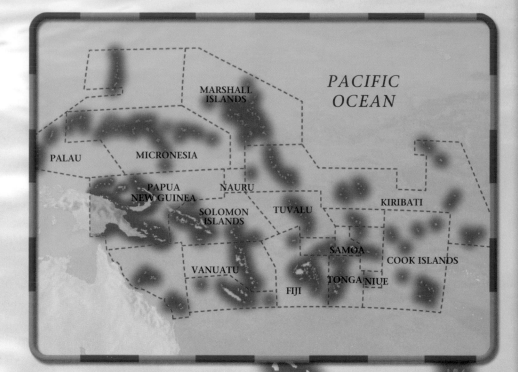

PACIFIC
OCEAN

MARSHALL
ISLANDS

PALAU

MICRONESIA

PAPUA
NEW GUINEA

NAURU

SOLOMON
ISLANDS

TUVALU

KIRIBATI

SAMOA

COOK ISLANDS

VANUATU

TONGA NIUE

FIJI

INDIAN
OCEAN

PACIFIC
OCEAN

AUSTRALIA

NEW
ZEALAND

SOUTHERN OCEAN

COUNTRY FACTFILE

Country	Life expectancy	Population in thousands	Population growth %	Population as urban %	Literacy %	Area km²	Population density per km²	Capital city	Currency	Languages
Australia	82	22,618	1.1	90	99	7,703,429	2.9	Canberra	Australian Dollar	English
Cook Islands	75	17.8	-3.0	75	95	237	75.1	Avarua	New Zealand Dollar	Cook Island Maori, English
Fiji	72	860	0.8	52	94	18,272	47.1	Suva	Fijian Dollar	English, Fijian
Kiribati	65	99	1.2	44	90	717	138.1	Bairiki	Australian Dollar	I-Kiribati, English
Marshall Islands	72	56	2	72	94	181	309.4	Majuro	US Dollar	Marshallese, English
Micronesia	72	103	-0.3	26	89	701	146.9	Palikir	US Dollar	English, Chuukese, Pohnpeain
Nauru	66	9.3	0.0	N/A	90	21	442.9	Yaren	Australian Dollar	Nauruan
New Zealand	81	4405	0.9	87	99	270,534	16.3	Wellington	New Zealand Dollar	English, Maori
Niue	75	1.6	-0.03	38	95	259	6.2	Alofi	New Zealand Dollar	Niuean, English
Palau	72	19.9	0.4	83	92	458	43.4	Ngerulmud-Melekeok	US Dollar	Palauan, English
Papua New Guinea	66	7060	2	17	17	462,840	15.3	Port Moresby	Kina	Tok Pisin (Pidgin English), English
Samoa	73	186	0.6	34	99	2831	65.7	Apia	Tala	Samoan
Solomon Islands	74	516	2.2	18	54	28,370	18.2	Honiara	Solmon Islands Dollar	Melanesian languages
Tonga	75	103	0.2	43	99	748	137.7	Nuku'alofa	Pa'anga	Tongan
Tuvalu	65	11	0.7	50	95	24	458.3	Vaiaku (Funafuti)	Australian Dollar	Melanesian languages
Vanuatu	65	243	1.3	26	74	12,190	19.9	Port-Vila	Vatu	Bislama, English, French

* Both the Cook Islands and Niue are self-governing states, but in free association with New Zealand, which is responsible for the aspects of foreign relations and defence that these countries agree to.

Australia

Much of Australia's inland is desert, known as the outback. Most people live in the eastern fertile land between Adelaide and Brisbane, and the capital, Canberra, is in the mountains of the Great Dividing Range. Many lakes in Australia vary in extent and some dry out in drought. Aboriginal people have lived in Australia for more than 40,000 years, but in 1787, British settlers began to arrive and immigration has continued ever since. Aboriginals now make up just 2 percent of the population. Rich in gold, iron ore and coal, Australia is one of the wealthiest nations in the world.

Extreme Weather

To fight the effects of long periods of drought, Toowoomba [F13] may use recycled sewage in the water supply.

Did You Know?

The Great Barrier Reef [D12] stretches for more than 2000 km off the coast of Queensland.

SYDNEY [H12] is the largest city and has two of the most famous sights in the world – the Opera House and Sydney Harbour Bridge.

THE DISTANCE from the east coast to the west coast is 3000 km – the same as from London to Boston, USA.

Facts and Stats

• Australia's area of 7.7 million km² is 75 times the area of Iceland.

• The Murray–Darling [H11] is the longest river. At 3750 km, it is more than half the length of the Nile river.

• Mount Kosciuszko [H11] is the highest mountain at 2229 m in height – seven times higher than the Eiffel Tower.

INDIAN OCEAN

Melvi Islan

Bathurst Island

Darwin

Joseph Bonaparte Gulf

Da

Drysdale

Wyndham

KIMBERLEY PLATEAU

Vic

Broome ●

● Derby
Fitzroy

● Halls Creek

● Port Hedland

GREAT SANDY DESERT

Dampier ●

De Grey

● Onslow

● Exmouth

Ashburton

NO

MA

● Carnarvon

WESTERN AUSTRALIA

GIBSON DESERT

Ayers Rock (Ulur

● Denham

Murchison

● Meekatharra

● Laverton

● Geraldton

GREAT VICTORIA DESERT

● Kalgoorlie

Balladonia ●

● Perth
● Freemantle
● Mandurah

● Norseman

Great Australi

Bunbury ●

● Wagin

● Esperance

Augusta ●

● Albany

SOUTHERN OCEAN

▷ *The widest bridge in the world, **Sydney Harbour Bridge** [H12] is almost 50 m in width. At 503 m in length, the bridge has two railway tracks, eight lanes for cars, a bicycle path and a pedestrian path. About 160,000 vehicles cross the bridge each day.*

A

RNHEM LAND

Groote Eylandt

Roper

herine

Gulf of Carpentaria

Cape York Peninsula

Kangaroos *can reach speeds of up to 50 km/h. They can be a danger on the roads, causing damage to vehicles in accidents as they weigh up to 90 kg. Therefore 'kangaroo crossing' signs are found throughout Australia.*

B

WELLESLEY ISLANDS

Mitchell

Cooktown •

• Port Doulgas

GREAT

Cairns •

Atherton •

• Innisfail

C

• Normanton

Burketown •

Flinders

• Tennant Creek

NAMI

ESERT

• Mount Isa

Norman

GREAT DIVIDING RANGE

BARRIER

REEF

• Townsville

Bowen •

PACIFIC OCEAN

D

ERN TERRITORY

Georgina

QUEENSLAND

• Mackay

• Alice Springs

Diamantina

Thomson

Barcoo

• Rockhampton

• Gladstone

ONNELL RANGES

AUSTRALIA

Charleville •

Warrego

Bundaberg •

Fraser Island

E

• Marla

Toowoomba •

• Sunshine Coast

• Brisbane

• Gold Coast

F

Coober Pedy •

OUTH AUSTRALIA

• Marree

Bourke •

Tamworth •

• Grafton

• Coffs Harbour

• Port Macquarie

Tarcoola •

NEW SOUTH WALES

Ceduna •

Darling

Dubbo •

GREAT DIVIDING RANGE

• Newcastle

• Gosford

G

ght

Port Augusta •

Whyalla •

• Port Pirie

Mildura •

Wagga Wagga •

• Sydney

• Wollongong

Port Lincoln •

Adelaide •

Murray

Canberra

AUSTRALIAN CAPITAL TERRITORY

H

Kangaroo Island

VICTORIA

Mount Kosciuszko 2229 m

Bendigo •

Ballarat •

• Melbourne

TASMAN SEA

Mount Gambier •

Geelong •

Sale •

I

King Island

Bass Strait

Flinders Island

Cape Barren Island

100 200 300 400 500 mi

200 400 600 800 km

Burnie •

• Devonport

• Launceston

Queenstown •

TASMANIA

• Hobart

South East Cape

New Zealand and the Pacific Islands

New Zealand consists of two main islands and has a population of four million. The country generates a wealthy economy, mainly by selling its farm produce worldwide. English is the national language due to the many immigrants who started commercial farms and industries. The area of the Pacific Ocean east of Australia contains thousands of tropical islands including the Solomon Islands, Fiji, Vanuatu, Samoa, Kiribati, Tonga, Micronesia, Palau, the Marshall Islands, Papua New Guinea, Nauru and Tuvalu. Many people are leaving the Pacific Islands for education and work in Australia, New Zealand and the USA.

Bora-Bora is a small island in French Polynesia [I14] with a population of only 8000 people. The biggest industry is tourism as people are attracted to the stunning clear waters and tranquil atmosphere. Resorts with bungalows on stilts are a common feature.

In the next ...New Zealand's wine growers will make more than 230 bottles of wine for export. **minute...**

THE DISTANCE from the top to the bottom of the Nevis Highwire, New Zealand's highest bungee jump, is 135 m.

OTAGO PENINSULA [I7] is home to albatrosses, penguins, seals, whales and dolphins.

Facts and Stats

• The life expectancy of people in New Zealand is 81 years, compared to a world average of 68 years.

• There are 24 doctors per 10,000 people compared to a world average of 17 doctors.

• Mount Cook [H7] is the highest mountain at 3754 m – 12 times higher than the Eiffel Tower.

The Maori were the first settlers in New Zealand, as they sailed from Polynesia 1000 years ago. Maori tikis are large carvings that are believed to protect sacred sites against evil.

TASMAN SEA

Cape Foulwind
Westport

Greymouth

Sou

Mount Cook 3754 m

SOUTHERN ALPS

Timaru

Waitaki

Oama

Otago Peninsu

Clutha

Dunedin

Cape Providence

Foveaux Strait • Invercargill

Codfish Island Ruapuke Island

Stewart Island

North Cape

Whangarei

Great Barrier Island

Hauraki Gulf

Auckland

Manukau

Waikato

Bay of Plenty

East Cape

Hamilton

Tauranga

Rotorua

North Island

Lake Taupo

New Plymouth

Mount Ruapehu 2797 m

Gisborne

Poverty Bay

Cape Egmont

Wanganui

Hawke Bay

Napier

Hastings

NEW ZEALAND

Wanganui

Cape Farewell

Palmerston North

Cook Strait

Lower Hutt

Wellington

Nelson

Blenheim

Cape Palliser

...land

...nterbury Bight

Christchurch

SOUTH PACIFIC OCEAN

▷ Rotorua [C10] is well-known for geothermal activity including geysers and mud pools. Each day, soap is put into the opening of **Lady Knox Geyser** to make it erupt. The jets of water can reach up to 20 m in height.

Search and Find

Cook Islands	. . . I13	Palau	. . . . . . H10
Fiji	. . . . I12	Papua New Guinea	
Kiribati	. . . . . H12		. . . . I11
Marshall Islands		Samoa	. . . . I13
	. . . . H12	Solomon Islands	
Micronesia	. . . H12		. . . . I12
Nauru	. . . . . H12	Tonga	. . . . . . I13
New Zealand		Tuvalu	. . . . . . I12
● Wellington	. . . . F9	Vanuatu	. . . . . . I12
Niue	. . . . I13		

Extreme Weather

The mountains of South Island have hurricane winds of more than 250 km/h.

Scale:
0 50 100 150 mi
0 100 200 km

Did You Know?

The sea level is rising due to global warming. Two South Pacific islands in Kiribati, Tebua Tarawa and Abanuea, have already disappeared.

PACIFIC OCEAN

NORTHERN MARIANA ISLANDS (US)

GUAM (US)

MARSHALL ISLANDS

PALAU

MICRONESIA

NAURU

TUVALU

KIRIBATI

PAPUA NEW GUINEA

SOLOMON ISLANDS

TOKELAU (NEW ZEALAND)

WALLIS AND FUTUNA (FRANCE)

SAMOA

AMERICAN SAMOA (US)

COOK ISLANDS

CORAL SEA ISLANDS TERRITORY (AUSTRALIA)

VANUATU

TONGA

NIUE

NEW CALEDONIA (FRANCE)

FIJI

FRENCH POLYNESIA (FRANCE)

Scale:
0 500 1000 mi
0 800 1600 km

Countries of the world

Gazetteer

The gazetteer helps you to find towns and features on the maps. For example, **New York City** *Town* New York, USA 21 F12 shows that New York City is a town in the state of New York, USA. The town is on page 21 and can be found in square F12 by using the grid, or graticule. The letters run on the left and right, and the numbers run along the top and bottom. Trace where F and 21 meet to find New York City.

KEY: DRC – Democratic Republic of the Congo, UAE – United Arab Emirates, CAR – Central African Republic, RS – Research station

Aachen *Town* Germany 50 F6
Aalst *Town* Belgium 50 E5
Abadan *Town* Iran 75 D8
Abakan *Town* Russian Fed. 86 H5
Abéché *Town* Chad 65 G13
Aberdeen *Town* Scotland, UK 41 D9
Aberdeen *Town* S Dakota, USA 25 F13
Aberystwyth *Town* Wales, UK 41 H8
Abha *Town* Saudi Arabia 74 H6
Abidjan *Capital* Côte d'Ivoire 64 I6
Abilene *Town* Texas, USA 27 G12
Abkhazia *State* Georgia 58 I7
Abu Dhabi *Capital* UAE 75 F10
Abuja *Capital* Nigeria 65 H10
Abu Kamal *Town* Syria 73 G12
Acapulco *Town* Mexico 31 I9
Acarigua *Town* Venezuela 35 F9
Accra *Capital* Ghana 64 I7
Aconcagua, Cerro *Mountain* Argentina 36 G7
Adana *Town* Turkey 73 E9
Ad-Dammam *Town* Saudi Arabia 75 E8
Addis Ababa *Capital* Ethiopia 67 E9
Adelaide *Town* Australia 91 H9
Aden, Gulf of 67 C12, 74 J7
Aden *Town* Yemen 74 J7
Adirondack Mountains USA 21 E11
Adiyaman *Town* Turkey 73 E11
Adrar *Town* Algeria 62 F4
Adriatic Sea 49 E8
Afghanistan *Country* 76
Agadir *Town* Morocco 62 E2
Agen *Town* France 46 G7
Agra *Town* India 77 D9
Agrigento *Town* Sicily, Italy 48 H6
Aguascalientes *Town* Mexico 31 G8
Ahaggar *Mountain range* Algeria 62 G6
Ahmadabad *Town* India 76 E7
Ahvaz *Town* Iran 75 D8
Aïr Mountains Niger 65 F10
Aix-en-Provence *Town* France 47 H10
Aizu *Town* Japan 83 F10
Ajaccio *Town* France 47 J12
Akita *Town* Japan 83 D10
Akron *Town* Ohio, USA 21 G8
Aktau *Town* Kazakhstan 86 I2
Alabama *River* Alabama, USA 23 F8

Alabama *State* USA 23
Åland Island Finland 43 G9
Alaska, Gulf of 25 C11, 28 F4
Alaska *State* USA 25
Albacete *Town* Spain 45 F10
Alba Iulia *Town* Romania 55 E9
Albania *Country* 49
Albany *River* Ontario, Canada 29 H10
Albany *State capital* New York, USA 21 E12
Albany *Town* Australia 90 H5
Albany *Town* Georgia, USA 23 F9
Albert, Lake DRC/Uganda 66 F7
Alberta *Province* Canada 28
Albuquerque *Town* New Mexico, USA 27 F9
Alcoy *Town* Spain 45 G11
Aleppo *Town* Syria 73 F10
Alessandria *Town* Italy 48 C5
Aleutian Islands Alaska, USA 25 C9
Alexandria *Town* Egypt 63 E12
Alexandria *Town* Louisiana, USA 22 G5
Alexandroúpolis *Town* Greece 49 F13
Algeciras *Town* Spain 44 I7
Algeria *Country* 62
Algiers *Capital* Algeria 62 C6
Al Hasakah *Town* Syria 73 F12
Al-Hudaydah *Town* Yemen 74 I6
Al-Hufuf *Town* Saudi Arabia 75 F8
Alicante *Town* Spain 45 G11
Alice Springs *Town* Australia 91 E8
Al Jawf *Town* Saudi Arabia 74 D5
Al-Karak *Town* Jordan 73 I9
Alkmaar *Town* Netherlands 50 C6
Allahabad *Town* India 77 E9
Allegheny *River* Pennsylvania, USA 21 G9
Allentown *Town* Pennsylvania, USA 21 G11
Almaty *Town* Kazakhstan 86 I4
Almería *Town* Spain 45 H9
Al Mukalla *Town* Yemen 75 I8
Alps *Mountain range* France/Italy/Switzerland 47 G10
Al Qamishli *Town* Syria 73 E12
Al Qunaytirah *Town* Syria 73 H9
Altai Mountains Mongolia/Russian Fed. 84 D7
Altamaha *River* Georgia, USA 23 F10

Altamira *Town* Brazil 37 B9
Altun Shan *Mountain range* China 84 F6
Amarillo *Town* Texas, USA 27 F11
Amazon *River* Brazil 36 B7, 37 B9
Amazon Basin Brazil 36 B7
Ambato *Town* Ecuador 36 B5
Ambon *Town* Indonesia 81 G8
American Samoa *Dep. territory* USA 93 I13
Amiens *Town* France 47 B9
Amman *Capital* Jordan 73 H10
Amritsar *Town* India 77 C8
Amsterdam *Capital* Netherlands 50 D6
Amu Dar'ya *River* Uzbekistan 86 J3
Amundsen Gulf 17 D9
Amundsen-Scott (US) *RS* Antarctica 16 F4
Amundsen Sea 16 F1
Amur *River* China/Russian Fed. 87 H8
Anaheim *Town* California, USA 26 F5
Anápolis *Town* Brazil 37 D9
Anatolian Plateau Turkey 72 D7
Anchorage *Town* Alaska, USA 25 C11
Ancona *Town* Italy 48 D7
Andaman Islands India 77 H12
Andaman Sea 78 H2
Anderson *Town* Indiana, USA 20 H7
Andes *Mountain range* 36 F7
Andorra *Country* 45
Andorra la Vella *Capital* Andorra 45 C12
Andreanof Islands Alaska, USA 25 C9
Angarsk *Town* Russian Fed. 86 H6
Angeles *Town* Philippines 79 F10
Angers *Town* France 46 C7
Angola *Country* 68
Angoulême *Town* France 46 E7
Anguilla *Dep. territory* UK 35 D12
Ankara *Capital* Turkey 73 C8
Annaba *Town* Algeria 62 D7
Annapolis *State capital* Maryland, USA 21 H11
Ann Arbor *Town* Michigan, USA 20 F7
An Nasiriyah *Town* Iraq 74 D7

Anshan *Town* China 85 D12
Antakya *Town* Turkey 73 F10
Antalya *Town* Turkey 72 E7
Antananarivo *Capital* Madagascar 69 G12
Antarctica 16
Antarctic Peninsula Antarctica 16 E2
Antibes *Town* France 47 H11
Anticosti Island Quebec, Canada 29 H13
Antigua and Barbuda *Country* 35
Antofagasta *Town* Chile 36 E6
Antsiranana *Town* Madagascar 69 F13
Antwerp *Town* Belgium 50 E5
Aomori *Town* Japan 83 D10
Aosta *Town* Italy 48 B4
Apeldoorn *Town* Netherlands 50 D7
Appalachian Mountains USA 21 H10, 23 C10
Appleton *Town* Wisconsin, USA 20 F5
Aqaba *Town* Jordan 73 J9
Aqtobe *Town* Russian Fed. 86 H2
Arabian Sea 75 F12, 76 E6
Aracaju *Town* Brazil 37 C11
Arad *Town* Romania 54 D7
Arafura Sea 81 H9
Araguaína *Town* Brazil 37 C10
Arakan Range *Mountain range* Burma (Myanmar) 78 F2
Aral Sea Kazakhstan/Uzbekistan 86 I3
Ararat, Mount Turkey 73 D14
Arbil *Town* Iraq 74 B7
Arctic Ocean 17, 28, 43, 59, 86
Arequipa *Town* Peru 36 D6
Arezzo *Town* Italy 48 D6
Argentina *Country* 36
Århus *Town* Denmark 42 I6
Arica *Town* Chile 36 D6
Arizona *State* USA 26
Arkansas *State* USA 22
Arkhangelsk *Town* Russian Fed. 59 D8
Arles *Town* France 47 H9
Arlington *Town* Texas, USA 27 G13
Armenia *Country* 59
Armenia *Town* Colombia 35 H8
Arnhem *Town* Netherlands 50 D6
Arnhem Land Australia 91 B8
Ar Raqqah *Town* Syria 73 F11

Arua *Town* Uganda 66 F7
Aruba *Dep. territory* Netherlands 35 E9
Aru Islands Indonesia 81 G9
Arusha *Town* Tanzania 67 H9
Asahikawa *Town* Japan 83 B10
Ashgabat *Capital* Turkmenistan 86 J3
Asmara *Capital* Eritrea 67 C9
Assad, Lake Syria 73 F11
Assen *Town* Netherlands 50 C7
As-Sulayyil *Town* Saudi Arabia 74 G7
Astana *Capital* Kazakhstan 86 H3
Astrakhan *Town* Russian Fed. 59 H8
Asunción *Capital* Paraguay 37 E8
Aswan *Town* Egypt 63 H13
Asyut *Town* Egypt 63 G13
Atacama Desert Chile 36 E7
Atbara *Town* Sudan 67 B8
Athens *Capital* Greece 49 H12
Atlanta *State capital* Georgia, USA 23 E9
Atlantic City *Town* New Jersey, USA 21 G12
Atlantic Ocean 21, 23, 29, 37, 40, 42, 43, 44, 62, 64
Atlas Mountains Morocco 62 E3
Atyrau *Town* Kazakhstan 86 I2
Auckland *Town* New Zealand 93 C9
Augsburg *Town* Germany 51 I9
Augusta *Town* Georgia, USA 23 E10
Augusta *State capital* Maine, USA 21 D13
Aurora *Town* Illinois, USA 20 G6
Austin *State capital* Texas, USA 27 H13
Australia *Country* 90
Australian Capital Territory *State* Australia 91
Austria *Country* 40
Auxerre *Town* France 47 D9
Aveiro *Town* Portugal 44 E5
Avignon *Town* France 47 G9
Ávila *Town* Spain 45 E8
Axel Heiberg Island Nunavut, Canada 29 C9
Ayacucho *Town* Peru 36 D6
Aydin *Town* Turkey 72 D6
Azerbaijan *Country* 59
Azov, Sea of 58 I7
Az-Zarqa *Town* Jordan 73 H10
Az-Zawiyah *Town* Libya 73 H10

Bacău *Town* Romania 55 D12
Bacolod *Town* Philippines 79 G11
Badajoz *Town* Spain 44 F6
Baden-Baden *Town* Germany 50 H7
Baffin Bay Canada 17 G9, 29 D10
Baffin Island Canada 17 G8, 29 E10

Baghdad *Capital* Iraq 74 C7
Bahamas *Country* 35
Bahawalpur *Town* Pakistan 77 C8
Bahía Blanca *Town* Argentina 37 G8
Bahrain *Country* 75
Baikal, Lake Russian Fed. 86 H7
Bakersfield *Town* California, USA 26 E5
Bakhtaran *Town* Iran 74 C7
Baku *Capital* Azerbaijan 59 J9
Balaton, Lake Hungary 54 D5
Balearic Islands Spain 45
Bali *Island* Indonesia 80 H5
Balikesir *Town* Turkey 72 C6
Balikpapan *Town* Indonesia 80 F5
Balkanabat *Town* Turkmenistan 86 J2
Balkan Mountains Bulgaria 55 H10
Balkhash, Lake Kazakhstan 86 I4
Ballarat *Town* Australia 91 I10
Baltic Sea 43 H9, 56 B6, 58 F5
Baltimore *Town* Maryland, USA 21 H11
Bamako *Capital* Mali 64 G5
Bambari *Town* CAR 68 B7
Bamberg *Town* Germany 51 G9
Bamenda *Town* Cameroon 68 B5
Bandar 'Abbas *Town* Iran 75 E10
Bandar Seri Begawan *Capital* Brunei 80 E5
Banda Sea 81 G8
Bandundu *Town* DRC 68 D7
Bandung *Town* Indonesia 80 H3
Bangalore *See Bengaluru*
Bangkok *Capital* Thailand 78 H4
Bangladesh *Country* 77
Bangor *Town* Maine, USA 21 C13
Bangui *Capital* CAR 68 B7
Baniyas *Town* Syria 73 F10
Banja Luka *Town* Bosnia and Herz. 49 C8
Banjarmasin *Town* Indonesia 80 G5
Banjul *Capital* Gambia 64 G3
Banská Bystrica *Town* Slovakia 57 I8
Baotou *Town* China 85 E10
Bar *Town* Montenegro 49 E9
Barbados *Country* 35
Barcelona *Town* Spain 45 D13
Barcelona *Town* Venezuela 35 F11
Barents Sea 17 G13, 58 B7
Bari *Town* Italy 49 F8
Barinas *Town* Venezuela 35 F9
Barnaul *Town* Russian Fed. 86 H5
Barquisimeto *Town* Venezuela 35 F9
Barrancabermeja *Town* Colombia 35 G8
Barranquilla *Town* Colombia 35 F8
Basel *Town* Switzerland 52 E3
Basra *Town* Iraq 75 D8

Bassein *Town* Burma (Myanmar) 78 G2
Basseterre *Capital* St. Kitts and Nevis 35 D12
Bass Strait Australia 91 I11
Batangas *Town* Philippines 79 F10
Batdâmbang *Town* Cambodia 78 G5
Batman *Town* Turkey 73 E12
Batna *Town* Algeria 62 D6
Baton Rouge *State capital* Louisiana, USA 22 G6
Bayamo *Town* Cuba 35 C8
Bayreuth *Town* Germany 51 G10
Beaufort Sea 17 C9, 28 D6
Beaumont *Town* Texas, USA 27 H14
Béchar *Town* Algeria 62 E4
Beersheba *Town* Israel 73 I9
Beijing *Capital* China 85 E11
Beira *Town* Mozambique 69 G10
Beirut *Capital* Lebanon 73 G9
Beja *Town* Portugal 44 G5
Belarus *Country* 58
Belém *Town* Brazil 37 B10
Belfast *Capital* Northern Ireland, UK 40 F7
Belgium *Country* 50
Belgrade *Capital* Serbia 49 C10
Belgrano II (Argentina) *RS* Antarctica 16 E3
Belize *Country* 34
Belize City *Town* Belize 34 C5
Bellingham *Town* Washington, USA 24 C4
Belmopan *Capital* Belize 34 C5
Belo Horizonte *Town* Brazil 37 E10
Bendigo *Town* Australia 91 H11
Benevento *Town* Italy 48 F7
Bengal, Bay of 77 F11
Bengaluru (Bangalore) *Town* India 77 H8
Benghazi *Town* Libya 63 E10
Benguela *Town* Angola 68 F6
Benidorm *Town* Spain 45 G11
Benin *Country* 65
Benin City *Town* Nigeria 65 I9
Ben Nevis *Mountain* Scotland, UK 41 D8
Benue *River* Nigeria 65 I10
Berbera *Town* Somalia 67 D11
Bergamo *Town* Italy 48 B5
Bergen *Town* Norway 42 F5
Bergerac *Town* France 46 F7
Bering Sea 25 B9, 87 G13
Berlin *Capital* Germany 51 D11
Bern *Capital* Switzerland 52 F3
Besançon *Town* France 47 E10
Bethlehem *Town* Israel 73 I9
Béziers *Town* France 47 H8
Bhavnagar *Town* India 76 E7

Bhopal *Town* India 77 E8
Bhutan *Country* 77
Bialystok *Town* Poland 57 D11
Biel *Town* Switzerland 52 F3
Bielefeld *Town* Germany 51 D8
Bielsko-Biala *Town* Poland 57 H8
Bighorn Mountains Wyoming, USA 25 G9
Bihac *Town* Bosnia and Herz. 49 C8
Bilauktaung Range Thailand 78 G3
Bilbao *Town* Spain 45 B9
Billings *Town* Montana, USA 25 F9
Biloxi *Town* Mississippi, USA 22 G7
Biratnagar *Town* Nepal 77 D11
Birmingham *Town* Alabama, USA 23 E8
Birmingham *Town* England, UK 41 H9
Biscay, Bay of 45 A9, 46 E5
Bishkek *Capital* Kyrgyzstan 86 I4
Bismarck *State capital* N Dakota, USA 25 F12
Bissau *Capital* Guinea-Bissau 64 G3
Bitola *Town* Macedonia 49 F11
Bizerte *Town* Tunisia 62 C7
Black Forest Germany 50 I7
Blackpool *Town* England, UK 41 F8
Black Sea 55 H14, 58 I6, 73 B11
Blagoevgrad *Town* Bulgaria 55 I9
Blagoveshchensk *Town* Russian Fed. 87 H8
Blantyre *Town* Malawi 69 G10
Blida *Town* Algeria 62 D6
Bloemfontein *Town* South Africa 69 I8
Bloomington *Town* Indiana, USA 20 I6
Bloomington *Town* Minnesota, USA 20 E3
Blue Nile *River* Ethiopia/Sudan 67 D8
Bo *Town* Sierra Leone 64 I4
Boa Vista *Town* Brazil 37 A8
Bobo Dioulasso *Town* Burkina Faso 64 H6
Bodrum *Town* Turkey 72 E5
Bogotá *Capital* Colombia 35 H8
Bohemian Forest Czech Republic/ Germany 51 H11, 56 H4
Boise *State capital* Idaho, USA 24 G5
Bolivia *Country* 36
Bologna *Town* Italy 48 C6
Bolzano *Town* Italy 48 B6
Bombay *See Mumbai*
Bonaire *Dep. territory* Netherlands 35 F10
Bonifacio, Strait of 47 J12
Bonn *Town* Germany 50 F7
Borås *Town* Sweden 42 H7

Bordeaux *Town* France 46 F6

Borgholm *Town* Sweden 43 I8

Borneo *Island* Indonesia 80 G4

Bornholm *Dep. territory* Denmark 42 J7

Bosnia and Herzegovina *Country* 49

Boston *State capital* Massachusetts, USA 21 E13

Botswana *Country* 69

Bouar *Town* CAR 68 B6

Boulder *Town* Colorado, USA 27 C10

Boulogne *Town* France 47 A9

Bourges *Town* France 47 D9

Bourke *Town* Australia 91 F11

Bournemouth *Town* England, UK 41 I9

Bozeman *Town* Montana, USA 25 F8

Brahmaputra *River* Asia 77 E12

Braila *Town* Romania 55 E12

Brandenburg *Town* Germany 51 D11

Brasília *Capital* Brazil 37 D10

Brasov *Town* Romania 55 E10

Bratislava *Capital* Slovakia 56 J7

Bratsk *Town* Russian Fed. 86 G6

Braunschweig *Town* Germany 51 D10

Brazil *Country* 37

Brazzaville *Capital* Republic of the Congo 68 D6

Breda *Town* Netherlands 50 D5

Bremen *Town* Germany 51 C9

Bremerhaven *Town* Germany 51 C8

Brescia *Town* Italy 48 B5

Brest *Town* France 46 B5

Bridgeport *Town* Connecticut, USA 21 F12

Bridgetown *Capital* Barbados 35 E12

Brig *Town* Switzerland 52 G3

Brighton *Town* England, UK 41 I10

Brindisi *Town* Italy 49 F9

Brisbane *Town* Australia 91 F13

Bristol *Town* England, UK 41 H9

British Columbia *Province* Canada 28

Brive *Town* France 47 F8

Brno *Town* Czech Republic 56 H6

Broome *Town* Australia 90 C5

Brownsville *Town* Texas, USA 27 J13

Bruges *Town* Belgium 50 E4

Brunei *Country* 80

Brussels *Capital* Belgium 50 E5

Bryansk *Town* Russian Fed. 58 G6

Bucaramanga *Town* Colombia 35 G8

Bucharest *Capital* Romania 55 F11

Budapest *Capital* Hungary 54 C6

Buenaventura *Town* Colombia 34 H7

Buenos Aires *Capital* Argentina 37 G8

Buffalo *Town* New York, USA 21 F9

Bug *River* Poland 57 D10

Bujumbura *Capital* Burundi 66 H7

Bukavu *Town* DRC 69 D9

Bulawayo *Town* Zimbabwe 69 G9

Bulgaria *Country* 55

Buraydah *Town* Saudi Arabia 74 E7

Burgas *Town* Bulgaria 55 H12

Burgos *Town* Spain 45 C8

Burketown *Town* Australia 91 C10

Burkina Faso *Country* 64

Burlington *Town* Vermont, USA 21 D12

Burma (Myanmar) *Country* 78

Burns *Town* Oregon, USA 24 G4

Burnsville *Town* Minnesota, USA 20 E3

Bursa *Town* Turkey 72 C6

Burundi *Country* 66

Butuan *Town* Philippines 79 G12

Bydgoszcz *Town* Poland 57 D8

Bytom *Town* Poland 57 G8

Cabanatuan *Town* Philippines 79 E10

Cáceres *Town* Spain 44 F6

Cádiz *Town* Spain 44 I7

Caen *Town* France 47 B8

Cagayan de Oro *Town* Philippines 79 G11

Cagliari *Town* Sardinia, Italy 48 G4

Cairns *Town* Australia 91 C11

Cairo *Capital* Egypt 63 F13

Calais *Town* France 47 A9

Calama *Town* Chile 36 E7

Calarasi *Town* Romania 55 F12

Calbayog *Town* Philippines 79 F11

Calcutta *See* Kolkata

Calgary *Town* Alberta, Canada 28 H7

Cali *Town* Colombia 34 H7

Calicut *See* Kozhikode

California, Gulf of 30 D5

California *State* USA 26

Callao *Town* Peru 36 D5

Caltanissetta *Town* Sicily, Italy 48 H7

Camagüey *Town* Cuba 35 C8

Cambodia *Country* 78

Cambrian Mountains Wales, UK 41 H8

Cambridge *Town* England, UK 41 H10

Cameroon *Country* 68

Campeche, Bay of Mexico 31 H11

Campina Grande *Town* Brazil 37 C12

Campinas *Town* Brazil 37 E10

Campobasso *Town* Italy 48 E7

Campo Grande *Town* Brazil 37 E9

Canada *Country* 28

Canary Islands Spain 64 B4

Canberra *Capital* Australia 91 H12

Cancún *Town* Mexico 31 G14

Cannes *Town* France 47 H11

Cantabrian Mountains Spain 44 B7

Can Tho *Town* Vietnam 78 H5

Canton *Town* Ohio, USA 21 G9

Cape Horn Chile 37 J8

Cape Town *Capital* South Africa 68 J7

Cape Verde *Country* 64

Cap-Haïtien *Town* Haiti 35 C9

Caracas *Capital* Venezuela 35 F10

Cárdenas *Town* Cuba 34 B7

Cardiff *Capital* Wales, UK 41 H8

Caribbean Sea 35 E9

Carlisle *Town* England, UK 41 F9

Carlsbad *Town* New Mexico, USA 27 G10

Carnarvon *Town* Australia 90 E3

Carpathian Mountains Poland/Romania/Slovakia 55 D11

Carrara *Town* Italy 48 C5

Carson City *State capital* Nevada, USA 26 C5

Cartagena *Town* Colombia 35 F8

Cartagena *Town* Spain 45 H11

Casablanca *Town* Morocco 62 D3

Casey (Australia) *RS* Antarctica 16 G7

Casper *Town* Wyoming, USA 25 H9

Caspian Sea 59 I9, 75 B8, 86 I2

Cassai (Kasai) *River* Angola/DRC 68 E7

Castellón de la Plana *Town* Spain 45 E11

Castries *Capital* St. Lucia 35 E12

Catania *Town* Sicily, Italy 48 H7

Catanzaro *Town* Italy 49 G8

Cayman Islands *Dep. territory* UK 34 C7

Cebu *Town* Philippines 79 G11

Cedar City *Town* Utah, USA 26 D7

Cedar Rapids *Town* Iowa, USA 20 G4

Celebes Sea 79 H11, 80 E6

Celje *Town* Slovenia 49 B8

Central African Republic (CAR) *Country* 68

Ceske Budejovice *Town* Czech Republic 56 H5

Ceuta *Town* Spain 44 J7, 62 D3

Chad, Lake Chad 65 G12

Chad *Country* 65

Châlons-en-Champagne *Town* France 47 C10

Chalon-sur-Saône *Town* France 47 E10

Chambéry *Town* France 47 F10

Champaign *Town* Illinois, USA 20 H6

Chandigarh *Town* India 77 C8

Chang Cheng (China) *RS* Antarctica 16 D1

Changchun *Town* China 85 C12

Chang Jiang (Yangtze) *River* China 85 G10

Changsha *Town* China 85 G11

Channel Islands *Dep. territory* UK 41 J9

Charleroi *Town* Belgium 50 F5

Charleston *State capital* West Virginia, USA 21 I9

Charleston *Town* S Carolina, USA 23 E11

Charleville Mézières *Town* France 47 B10

Charlotte *Town* N Carolina, USA 23 C10

Charlottetown *Province capital* Prince Edward Islands, Canada 29 I13

Châteauroux *Town* France 47 D8

Chattanooga *Town* Tennessee, USA 23 D8

Cheb *Town* Czech Republic 56 G3

Chelm *Town* Poland 57 F11

Chelyabinsk *Town* Russian Fed. 86 G3

Chemnitz *Town* Germany 51 F11

Chengdu *Town* China 85 G9

Chennai (Madras) *Town* India 77 H9

Chester *Town* England, UK 41 G9

Chetumal *Town* Mexico 31 H13

Cheyenne *State capital* Wyoming, USA 25 I10

Chiang Mai *Town* Thailand 78 F3

Chiba *Town* Japan 83 G10

Chicago *Town* Illinois, USA 20 G6

Chichén Itzá Mexico 31 G13

Chiclayo *Town* Peru 36 C5

Chicoutimi *Town* Quebec, Canada 29 I12

Chihuahua *Town* Mexico 30 D7

Chile *Country* 36

Chillan *Town* Chile 36 G6

Chilpancingo *Town* Mexico 31 I9

Chimbote *Town* Peru 36 C5

Chimoio *Town* Mozambique 69 G10

China *Country* 85

Chinandega *Town* Nicaragua 34 E5

Chioggia *Town* Italy 48 C6

Chipata *Town* Zambia 69 F9

Chirripó Grande, Cerro *Mountain* Costa Rica 34 F5

Chisinau *Capital* Moldova 58 H6

Chita *Town* Russian Fed. 86 H7

Chitose *Town* Japan 83 B10

Chittagong *Town* Bangladesh 77 F12

Chitungwiza *Town* Zimbabwe 69 G9

Chon Buri *Town* Thailand 78 H4

Chongjin *Town* North Korea 85 C13

Chongqing *Town* China 85 H10

Choybalsan *Town* Mongolia 85 C10

Christchurch *Town* New Zealand 93 G8

Chukchi Sea 17 C11, 25 A10, 87 E13

Churchill *Town* Manitoba, Canada 29 G9

Cienfuegos *Town* Cuba 34 B7

Cincinnati *Town* Ohio, USA 21 H7

Ciudad Bolívar *Town* Venezuela 35 G11

Ciudad del Este *Town* Paraguay 37 F9

Ciudad Guayana *Town* Venezuela 35 G11

Ciudad Juárez *Town* Mexico 30 C7

Ciudad Madero *Town* Mexico 31 F10

Ciudad Obregón *Town* Mexico 30 D6

Ciudad Real *Town* Spain 45 F8

Ciudid Victoria *Town* Mexico 31 F9

Civitavecchia *Town* Italy 48 E6

Clarksville *Town* Tennessee, USA 22 C7

Clearwater *Town* Florida, USA 23 H10

Clermont-Ferrand *Town* France 47 E9

Cleveland *Town* Ohio, USA 21 G8

Clovis *Town* New Mexico, USA 27 F11

Cluj-Napoca *Town* Romania 55 D9

Coast Ranges California/Oregon, USA 24 F2, 26 B4

Coatzacoalcos *Town* Mexico 31 H11

Cochin *See Kochi*

Cognac *Town* France 46 E7

Coimbatore *Town* India 77 I8

Coimbra *Town* Portugal 44 E5

Colchester *Town* England, UK 41 H10

Colima *Town* Mexico 31 H8

Cologne *Town* Germany 50 E7

Colombia *Country* 35

Colombo *Capital* Sri Lanka 77 J9

Colón *Town* Panama 34 F7

Colorado *River* Mexico/USA 27 D8

Colorado *State* USA 27

Colorado Springs *Town* Colorado, USA 27 D10

Columbia *State capital* S Carolina, USA 23 D10

Columbia *Town* Missouri, USA 22 B5

Columbus *State capital* Ohio, USA 21 H8

Columbus *Town* Georgia, USA 23 F9

Como *Town* Italy 48 B5

Comodoro Rivadavia *Town* Argentina 36 H7

Comoros *Country* 69

Conakry *Capital* Guinea 64 H4

Concepción *Town* Chile 36 G6

Concord *State capital* New Hampshire, USA 21 E13

Congo *River* Western Central Africa 68 C7, 69 D8

Congo, Democratic Republic of the (DRC) *Country* 68

Congo, Republic of the *Country* 68

Connecticut *State* USA 21

Constanta *Town* Romania 55 F13

Constantine *Town* Algeria 62 D6

Coober Pedy *Town* Australia 91 F8

Cook, Mount New Zealand 92 G7

Cook Islands *Dep. territory* New Zealand 93 I13

Cook Strait New Zealand 93 F9

Cooktown *Town* Australia 91 B11

Copenhagen *Capital* Denmark 42 I7

Coquimbo *Town* Chile 36 F6

Coral Sea Islands Territory *Dep. territory* Australia 93 I11

Cordillera Central *Mountain range* Colombia/Panama 34 F6, 35 H8

Córdoba *Town* Argentina 36 F7

Córdoba *Town* Spain 45 G8

Corfu *Island* Greece 49 G10

Cork *Town* Republic of Ireland 40 H6

Corpus Christi *Town* Texas, USA 27 I13

Corrientes *Town* Argentina 37 F8

Corsica *Island* France 47 I12

Çorum *Town* Turkey 73 C9

Corvallis *Town* Oregon, USA 24 F3

Cosenza *Town* Italy 49 G8

Costa Rica *Country* 34

Côte d'Ivoire *Country* 64

Cotonou *Capital* Benin 65 I8

Cottbus *Town* Germany 51 E12

Council Bluffs *Town* Iowa, USA 20 H2

Coventry *Town* England, UK 41 H9

Craiova *Town* Romania 55 G9

Cremona *Town* Italy 48 C5

Crete, Sea of Greece 49 I12

Crete *Island* Greece 49 J12

Crimea Ukraine 58 I7

Croatia *Country* 49

Crotone *Town* Italy 49 G8

Cuba *Country* 34

Cúcuta *Town* Colombia 35 G8

Cuernavaca *Town* Mexico 31 H9

Cuito *River* Angola 68 G7

Culiacán *Town* Mexico 30 E6

Cumaná *Town* Venezuela 35 F11

Curaçao *Dep. territory* Netherlands 35 E10

Curitiba *Town* Brazil 37 F9

Cusco *Town* Peru 36 D6

Cuttack *Town* India 77 F10

Cuxhaven *Town* Germany 51 B9

Cyprus *Country* 73

Czech Republic Country 56

Czestochowa *Town* Poland 57 F8

Dakar *Capital* Senegal 64 F3

Dalandzadgad *Town* Mongolia 85 D8

Da Lat *Town* Vietnam 78 H6

Dalian *Town* China 85 E12

Dallas *Town* Texas, USA 27 G13

Damascus *Capital* Syria 73 H10

Dampier *Town* Australia 90 D4

Da Nang *Town* Vietnam 78 F6

Danube *River* Europe 51 I8, 40 E12, 54 D5, 55 G10, 57 J8

Danzig, Gulf of 57 B8

Dar'a *Town* Syria 73 H10

Dar es Salaam *Capital* Tanzania 67 I9

Darfur Sudan 66 D6

Darhan *Town* Mongolia 85 C9

Darien, Gulf of 34 F7

Darling *River* Australia 91 G10

Darmstadt *Town* Germany 51 G8

Darnah *Town* Libya 63 E10

Darwin *Town* Australia 90 B7

Davao *Town* Philippines 79 H12

Davenport *Town* Iowa, USA 20 G5

David *Town* Panama 34 F6

Davis (Australia) *RS* Antarctica 16 E7

Dayr az Zawr *Town* Syria 73 F12

Dayton *Town* Ohio, USA 21 H8

Daytona Beach *Town* Florida, USA 23 G11

Dead Sea Jordan 73 I9

Death Valley California, USA 26 E6

Debrecen *Town* Hungary 55 C8

Decatur *Town* Illinois, USA 20 H6

Delaware *State* USA 21

Delft *Town* Netherlands 50 D5

Delhi *Town* India 77 D9

Del Rio *Town* Texas, USA 27 I11

Democratic Republic of the Congo (DRC) *See* Congo, Republic of the

Den Helder *Town* Netherlands 50 C6

Denizli *Town* Turkey 72 D6

Denmark *Country* 42

Denver *State capital* Colorado, USA 27 C10

Derby *Town* England, UK 41 G9

Des Moines *State capital* Iowa, USA 20 G3

Dessau *Town* Germany 51 E11

Detroit *Town* Michigan, USA 20 F8

Devon Island Nunavut, Canada 29 D9

Dhaka *Capital* Bangladesh 77 E11

Dhanbad *Town* India 77 E10

Dieppe *Town* France 47 B8

Dijon *Town* France 47 D10

Dili *Capital* East Timor 80 H7

Dimitrovgrad *Town* Bulgaria 55 I11

Dire Dawa *Town* Ethiopia 67 D10

Diyarbakir *Town* Turkey 73 E12

Djibouti *Capital* Djibouti 67 D11

Djibouti *Country* 67

Dnieper *River* Ukraine 58 H6

Dniester *River* Ukraine 58 H6

Dnipropetrovsik *Town* Ukraine 58 H7

Dobrich *Town* Bulgaria 55 G13

Dodge City *Town* Kansas, USA 27 E12

Dodoma *Capital* Tanzania 67 I9

Doha *Capital* Qatar 75 F9

Dominica *Country* 35

Dominican Republic *Country* 35

Don *River* Russian Fed. 59 H8

Donetsk *Town* Ukraine 58 H7

Dordogne *River* France 46 F7

Dordrecht *Town* Netherlands 50 D5

Dortmund *Town* Germany 50 E7

Douala *Town* Cameroon 68 B5

Douglas *Town* Arizona, USA 27 G8

Dover *State capital* Delaware, USA 21 G12

Dover *Town* England, UK 41 I11

Drakensberg Mountains South Africa 69 J8

Drama *Town* Greece 49 F12

Drammen *Town* Norway 42 G6

Dresden *Town* Germany 51 F12

Drobeta-Turnu Severin *Town* Romania 55 F8

Drogheda *Town* Republic of Ireland 40 F7

Dubai *Town* UAE 75 F10

Dublin *Capital* Republic of Ireland 40 G7

Dubrovnik *Town* Croatia 49 E9

Duisburg *Town* Germany 50 E7

Duluth *Town* Minnesota, USA 20 D3

Dumont d'Urville (France) *RS* Antarctica 16 H5

Dunaujvaros *Town* Hungary 54 D6

Dundee *Town* Scotland, UK 41 D9

Dunedin *Town* New Zealand 92 I7
Dunkerque *Town* France 47 A9
Durango *Town* Colorado, USA 27 E9
Durango *Town* Mexico 30 F7
Durban *Town* South Africa 69 I9
Durham *Town* N Carolina, USA
 23 C11
Durrës *Town* Albania 49 F9
Dushanbe *Capital* Tajikistan 86 J3
Düsseldorf *Town* Germany 50 E7

East Cape New Zealand 93 C11
East China Sea Pacific Ocean
 85 G13
Eastern Ghats *Mountain range*
 India 77 G9
East London *Town* South Africa
 69 J8
East Siberian Sea Arctic Ocean
 17 C13, 87 E11
East Timor *Country* 81
Eau Claire *Town* Wisconsin, USA
 20 E4
Ebetsu *Town* Japan 83 B10
Ebro *River* Spain 45 C10
Ecuador *Country* 36
Edinburgh *Capital* Scotland, UK
 41 E8
Edirne *Town* Turkey 72 B5
Edmonton *Province capital* Alberta,
 Canada 28 H7
Edward, Lake DRC/Uganda 66 G7,
 69 C9
Edwards Plateau Texas, USA 27 H12
Egypt *Country* 63
Eindhoven *Town* Netherlands 50 E6
El Aaiún *Capital* Western Sahara
 64 C5
Elat *Town* Israel 73 J9
Elazig *Town* Turkey 73 D11
Elbasan *Town* Albania 49 F10
Elbe *River* Czech Republic/ Germany
 51 E11, 56 G6
Elblag *Town* Poland 57 B8
Elbrus, Mount Russian Fed. 59 I8
Elche *Town* Spain 45 G11
El Fasher *Town* Sudan 66 C6
Elgin *Town* Illinois, USA 20 G6
Ellesmere Island Canada 17 F10,
 29 C9
Ellsworth Land Antarctica 16 F2
El Minya *Town* Egypt 63 F13
El Obeid *Town* Sudan 66 D7
El Paso *Town* Texas, USA 27 G9
El Progreso *Town* Honduras 34 D5
El Salvador *Country* 34
Emmen *Town* Netherlands 50 C7
Empty Quarter *Desert* Saudi Arabia
 75 H9
Ende *Town* Indonesia 80 H6

England *Country* UK 41
English Channel France/UK 41 I9,
 46 A6
Enid *Town* Oklahoma, USA 27 E13
Enschede *Town* Netherlands 50 D7
Ensenada *Town* Mexico 30 B4
Enugu *Town* Nigeria 65 I10
Equatorial Guinea *Country* 68
Erdenet *Town* Mongolia 85 C9
Erfurt *Town* Germany 51 F10
Erie, Lake USA 21 F9
Erie *Town* Pennsylvania, USA 21 F9
Eritrea *Country* 67
Erzincan *Town* Turkey 73 D11
Erzurum *Town* Turkey 73 C13
Esbjerg *Town* Denmark 42 I5
Escuintla *Town* Guatemala 34 D4
Esfahan *Town* Iran 75 C9
Eskisehir *Town* Turkey 72 C7
Esmeraldas *Town* Ecuador 36 A5
Esperance *Town* Australia 90 H6
Esperanza (Argentina) *RS*
 Antarctica 16 D1
Espoo *Town* Finland 43 G10
Essen *Town* Germany 50 E7
Estonia *Country* 58
Ethiopia *Country* 67
Etna, Mount Italy 48 H7
Eugene *Town* Oregon, USA 24 F3
Euphrates *River* Iraq/Syria/Turkey 73
 F12, 74 C8
Evansville *Town* Indiana, USA 20 J6
Everest, Mount China/Nepal
 77 D11, 84 H6
Everett *Town* Washington, USA
 24 D4
Everglades, The Florida, USA 23 J11
Évora *Town* Portugal 44 G5
Exeter *Town* England, UK 41 I8

Fairbanks *Town* Alaska, USA 25 B11
Faisalabad *Town* Pakistan 77 C8
Falkland Islands *Dep. territory* UK
 37 J8
Fargo *Town* N Dakota, USA 25 F13
Fayetteville *Town* N Carolina, USA
 23 C11
Feira de Santana *Town* Brazil
 37 D11
Ferrara *Town* Italy 48 C6
Fes *Town* Morocco 62 D3
Feuilles *River* Quebec, Canada
 29 G11
Fianarantsoa *Town* Madagascar
 69 H12
Fiji *Country* 93 I12
Finland, Gulf of 58 E5
Finland *Country* 43
Firat *River* Turkey 73 E11
Fitzroy *River* Australia 90 C6

Flagstaff *Town* Arizona, USA 27 F8
Flensburg *Town* Germany 51 A9
Flint *Town* Michigan, USA 20 F7
Florence *Town* Italy 48 D6
Flores Sea 80 H6
Florianópolio *Town* Brazil 37 F9
Florida *State* USA 23
Florida Keys *Island group* Florida,
 USA 23 J11
Focsani *Town* Romania 55 E12
Foggia *Town* Italy 49 E8
Fontainebleau *Town* France 47 C9
Forli *Town* Italy 48 C6
Fort Albany *Town* Ontario, Canada
 29 H10
Fortaleza *Town* Brazil 37 B11
Fort Collins *Town* Colorado, USA
 27 C10
Fort Lauderdale *Town* Florida, USA
 23 I12
Fort Myers *Town* Florida, USA 23 I11
Fort Smith *Town* Arkansas, USA
 22 D4
Fort Wayne *Town* Indiana, USA
 20 G7
Fort Worth *Town* Texas, USA 27 G13
Foveaux Strait New Zealand 92 J5
Fox Islands Alaska, USA 25 C9
France *Country* 46
Francistown *Town* Botswana 69 H8
Frankfurt am Main *Town* Germany
 51 G8
Frankfurt an der Oder *Town*
 Germany 51 D12
Fraser Island Australia 91 E13
Fredericton *Province capital* New
 Brunswick, Canada 29 I13
Fredrikstad *Town* Norway 42 G6
Freemantle *Town* Australia 90 G4
Freetown *Capital* Sierra Leone
 64 H4
Freiburg im Breisgau *Town*
 Germany 50 I7
French Guiana *Dep. territory* France
 35 H14
French Polynesia *Dep. territory*
 France 93 I14
Fresno *Town* California, USA 26 D5
Fuji, Mount Japan 83 G9
Fuji *Town* Japan 83 G9
Fukui *Town* Japan 83 G8
Fukuoka *Town* Japan 82 H5
Fukushima *Town* Japan 83 F10
Fulda *Town* Germany 51 F9
Fürth *Town* Germany 51 H9
Fushun *Town* China 85 D12
Fuzhou *Town* China 85 H12

Gabon *Country* 68
Gaborone *Capital* Botswana 69 H8

Gabrovo *Town* Bulgaria 55 H11
Gainesville *Town* Florida, USA
 23 G10
Gallup *Town* New Mexico, USA
 27 E9
Galveston *Town* Texas, USA 27 I14
Galway *Town* Republic of Ireland
 40 G6
Gambia *Country* 64
Gander *Town* Newfoundland and
 Labrador, Canada 29 H14
Ganges *River* India 77 D9
Gao *Town* Mali 65 F8
Gar *Town* China 84 G5
Garland *Town* Texas, USA 27 G13
Garonne *River* France 46 F7
Garoua *Town* Cameroon 68 A6
Gary *Town* Indiana, USA 20 G6
Gaspé *Town* Quebec, Canada
 29 H13
Gävle *Town* Sweden 43 G8
Gaza *Town* Israel 73 I9
Gaza Strip *Disputed region*
 Near East 73 I9
Gaziantep *Town* Turkey 73 E10
Gdansk *Town* Poland 57 B8
Gdynia *Town* Poland 57 B8
Geelong *Town* Australia 91 I11
General Santos *Town* Philippines 79
 H12
Geneva, Lake Switzerland 52 G1
Geneva *Town* Switzerland 52 G1
Genk *Town* Belgium 50 E6
Genoa *Town* Italy 48 C5
Georgetown *Capital* Guyana
 35 G13
George Town *Town* Malaysia
 80 E2
Georgia *Country* 59
Georgia *State* USA 23
Gera *Town* Germany 51 F10
Germany *Country* 50
Ghana *Country* 64
Ghardaïa *Town* Algeria 62 E6
Ghent *Town* Belgium 50 E5
Gibraltar *Dep. territory* UK 44 I7
Gibraltar, Strait of Morocco/Spain
 44 I7, 62 C3
Gibson Desert Australia 90 E5
Giessen *Town* Germany 51 F8
Gifu *Town* Japan 83 G8
Gijón *Town* Spain 44 B7
Gillette *Town* Wyoming, USA 25 G10
Girona *Town* Spain 45 C13
Gisborne *Town* New Zealand
 93 D11
Giurgiu *Town* Romania 55 G11
Glasgow *Town* Scotland, UK
 41 E8
Gliwice *Town* Poland 57 G8

Gloucester *Town* England, UK 41 H9
Gobi Desert Mongolia 85 D9
Godavari *River* India 77 F9
Godoy Cruz *Town* Argentina 36 G7
Goiânia *Town* Brazil 37 D9
Golan Heights *Mountain range* Syria 73 H9
Golmud *Town* China 84 F7
Gómez Palacio *Town* Mexico 31 E8
Gonaïves *Town* Haiti 35 C9
Gonder *Town* Ethiopia 67 D9
Gore *Town* Ethiopia 67 E9
Gorgan *Town* Iran 75 B9
Görlitz *Town* Germany 51 F12
Gorzow Wielkopolski *Town* Poland 56 D6
Gosford *Town* Australia 91 G12
Göteborg *Town* Sweden 42 H6
Gotland *Island* Sweden 43 H8
Göttingen *Town* Germany 51 E9
Gouda *Town* Netherlands 50 D6
Governador Valadares *Town* Brazil 37 E10
Grafton *Town* Australia 91 F13
Grampian Mountains Scotland, UK 41 D8
Granada *Town* Spain 45 H9
Gran Chaco Argentina 36 F7
Grand Canyon Arizona, USA 26 E7
Grand Forks *Town* N Dakota, USA 25 E13
Grand Rapids *Town* Michigan, USA 20 F7
Graz *Town* Austria 40 G12
Great Australian Bight Australia 90 G7
Great Barrier Island New Zealand 93 B9
Great Barrier Reef Australia 91 C12
Great Basin Nevada, USA 26 D6
Great Dividing Range Australia 91 D12
Great Falls *Town* Montana, USA 25 E8
Great Karoo South Africa 68 J7
Great Rift Valley Kenya 67 F9
Great Sandy Desert Australia 90 D6
Great Victoria Desert Australia 90 G5
Greece *Country* 49
Greeley *Town* Colorado, USA 27 C10
Green Bay *Town* Wisconsin, USA 20 E5
Greenland Sea 17 H11, 43 G12
Greensboro *Town* N Carolina, USA 23 C11
Greenville *Town* Mississippi, USA 22 E6
Greenville *Town* S Carolina, USA 23 D10

Greifswald *Town* Germany 51 B12
Grenada *Country* 35
Grenoble *Town* France 47 F10
Greymouth *Town* New Zealand 92 G7
Groningen *Town* Netherlands 50 C7
Grootfontein *Town* Namibia 68 G7
Grosseto *Town* Italy 48 D6
Grozny *Town* Russian Fed. 59 I8
Guadalajara *Town* Mexico 31 G8
Guadalajara *Town* Spain 45 E9
Guadeloupe *Dep. territory* France 35 D12
Guam *Dep. territory* USA 93 H11
Guanabacoa *Town* Cuba 34 B7
Guanare *Town* Venezuela 35 F9
Guangzhou *Town* China 85 I11
Guantánamo *Town* Cuba 35 C8
Guatemala *Country* 34
Guatemala City *Capital* Guatemala 34 D4
Guayaquil *Town* Ecuador 36 B5
Guaymas *Town* Mexico 30 D5
Guernsey *Island* Channel Islands, UK 41 J9
Guiana Highlands *Mountain range* Guyana/Venezuela 35 G12
Guinea, Gulf of 64 J7
Guinea *Country* 64
Guinea-Bissau *Country* 64
Guiyang *Town* China 85 H10
Gujranwala *Town* Pakistan 77 C8
Guwahati *Town* India 77 E12
Guyana *Country* 35
Gwadar *Town* Pakistan 76 D5
Gyor *Town* Hungary 54 C5

Haarlem *Town* Netherlands 50 D6
Hachinohe *Town* Japan 83 D10
Hadera *Town* Israel 73 H9
Haifa *Town* Israel 73 H9
Haikou *Town* China 85 J11
Hailar *Town* China 85 B11
Haiphong *Town* Vietnam 78 E5
Haiti *Country* 35
Hakodate *Town* Japan 83 C10
Halifax *Province capital* Nova Scotia, Canada 29 I13
Halle *Town* Germany 51 E10
Halley (UK) *RS* Antarctica 16 D3
Halmstad *Town* Sweden 42 I7
Hamadan *Town* Iran 75 C8
Hamah *Town* Syria 73 F10
Hamamatsu *Town* Japan 83 G9
Hamar *Town* Norway 42 G6
Hamburg *Town* Germany 51 C9
Hamhung *Town* North Korea 85 D13
Hamilton *Town* New Zealand 93 C9

Hamilton *Town* Ontario, Canada 29 J11
Hamm *Town* Germany 51 E8
Hanamaki *Town* Japan 83 E10
Hangzhou *Town* China 85 G12
Hannover *Town* Germany 51 D9
Hanoi *Capital* Vietnam 78 E5
Harare *Capital* Zimbabwe 69 G9
Harbel *Town* Liberia 64 I5
Harbin *Town* China 85 C12
Harer *Town* Ethiopia 67 E10
Hargeisa *Town* Somalia 67 D11
Harrisburg *State capital* Pennsylvania, USA 21 G11
Hartford *State capital* Connecticut, USA 21 F12
Hasselt *Town* Belgium 50 E6
Hastings *Town* New Zealand 93 E10
Hat Yai *Town* Thailand 78 J4
Haugesund *Town* Norway 42 G5
Havana *Capital* Cuba 34 B7
Hawaii *State* USA 26
Hefei *Town* China 85 F12
Heidelberg *Town* Germany 51 G8
Heilbronn *Town* Germany 51 H8
Helena *State capital* Montana, USA 24 E7
Helsingborg *Town* Sweden 42 I7
Helsinki *Capital* Finland 43 G10
Hengyang *Town* China 85 H11
Henzada *Town* Burrma (Myanmar) 78 F2
Herat *Town* Afghanistan 76 A6
Hermosillo *Town* Mexico 30 D5
Hilversum *Town* Netherlands 50 D6
Himalayas Asia 77 D10, 84 H6
Hims *Town* Syria 73 G10
Hirosaki *Town* Japan 83 D10
Hiroshima *Town* Japan 82 H6
Hitachi *Town* Japan 83 F10
Hobart *Town* Australia 91 J11
Ho Chi Minh City *Town* Vietnam 78 H6
Hofu *Town* Japan 82 H6
Hohhot *Town* China 85 E10
Hokkaido *Island* Japan 83 B11
Holguín *Town* Cuba 35 C8
Homyel *Town* Belarus 58 G6
Honduras *Country* 34
Hong Kong *Town* China 85 I11
Honolulu *State capital* Hawaii, USA 26 H3
Honshu *Island* Japan 83 F9
Hormuz, Strait of Iran/Oman 75 E10
Houston *Town* Texas, USA 27 H14
Hradec Kralove *Town* Czech Republic 56 G6
Hrodna *Town* Belarus 58 G5
Huacho *Town* Peru 36 C5
Huambo *Town* Angola 68 F6

Huancayo *Town* Peru 36 D6
Huang *River* China 85 F11
Hudson Bay Canada 29 G10
Hué *Town* Vietnam 78 F6
Huelva *Town* Spain 44 H6
Hull *Town* England, UK 41 F10
Hungary *Country* 54
Huntington *Town* West Virginia, USA 21 I9
Huntsville *Town* Alabama, USA 23 D8
Huron, Lake USA 20 E8
Hyderabad *Town* India 77 G8
Hyderabad *Town* Pakistan 76 D7
Hyesan *Town* North Korea 85 D13

Iasi *Town* Romania 55 C12
Ibadan *Town* Nigeria 65 I9
Ibagué *Town* Colombia 35 H8
Ibarra *Town* Ecuador 36 A5
Ibiza Balearic Islands, Spain 45 F12
Ibiza *Town* Ibiza, Spain 45 F12
Ica *Town* Peru 36 D5
Iceland *Country* 43
Idaho *State* USA 24
Idaho Falls *Town* Idaho, USA 24 G7
Illinois *River* Illinois, USA 20 H5
Illinois *State* USA 20
Iloilo *Town* Philippines 79 G11
Ilorin *Town* Nigeria 65 I9
Imperatriz *Town* Brazil 37 B10
Imphal *Town* India 77 E12
Inchon *Town* South Korea 85 E13
Independence *Town* Missouri, USA 22 B4
India *Country* 77
Indiana *State* USA 20
Indianapolis *State capital* Indiana, USA 20 H7
Indian Ocean 67, 69, 76, 90
Indonesia *Country* 80
Indore *Town* India 77 E8
Indus *River* Pakistan 76 D7
Ingolstadt *Town* Germany 51 H10
Inhambane *Town* Mozambique 69 H10
Innsbruck *Town* Austria 52 F7
In Salah *Town* Algeria 62 F5
Invercargill *Town* New Zealand 92 J6
Inverness *Town* Scotland, UK 41 C8
Ioánnina *Town* Greece 49 G10
Ionian Sea 49 H9
Iowa *State* USA 20
Ipoh *Town* Malaysia 80 E2
Ipswich *Town* England, UK 41 H10
Iqaluit *Province capital* Nunavut, Canada 29 F11
Iquique *Town* Chile 36 E6
Iquitos *Town* Peru 36 B6
Iráklion *Town* Crete, Greece 49 I12

Iran *Country* 75
Iraq *Country* 74
Irbid *Town* Jordan 73 H9
Ireland, Republic of *Country* 40
Iringa *Town* Tanzania 67 I9
Irish Sea 40 F7
Irkutsk *Town* Russian Fed. 86 H6
Irrawaddy *River* Burma (Myanmar) 78 F2
Ishinomaki *Town* Japan 83 E10
Islamabad *Capital* Pakistan 77 B8
Isle of Man *Dep. territory* UK 41 F8
Isparta *Town* Turkey 72 E7
Israel *Country* 73
Istanbul *Town* Turkey 72 B6
Itabuna *Town* Brazil 37 D11
Italy *Country* 48
Iwaki *Town* Japan 83 F10
Izhevsk *Town* Russian Fed. 59 F9
Izmir *Town* Turkey 72 D5
Izmit *Town* Turkey 72 C7

Jackson *State capital* Mississippi, USA 22 F6
Jacksonville *Town* Florida, USA 23 G10
Jaén *Town* Spain 45 H8
Jaffna *Town* Sri Lanka 77 I9
Jaipur *Town* India 77 D8
Jakarta *Capital* Indonesia 80 H3
Jamaica *Country* 35
Jambi *Town* Indonesia 80 F2
Jamnagar *Town* India 76 E7
Jamshedpur *Town* India 77 E10
Janesville *Town* Wisconsin, USA 20 G5
Japan, Sea of 82 F7, 85 D13
Japan *Country* 82
Java *Island* Indonesia 80 H4
Java Sea 80 H4
Jayapura *Town* Indonesia 81 F11
Jefferson City *State capital* Missouri, USA 22 B5
Jena *Town* Germany 51 F10
Jersey *Island* Channel Islands, UK 41 J9
Jerusalem *Capital* Israel 73 I9
Jiddah *Town* Saudi Arabia 74 G5
Jihlava *Town* Czech Republic 56 H6
Jilin *Town* China 85 C12
Jima *Town* Ethiopia 67 E9
Jinan *Town* China 85 E11
Jinzhou *Town* China 85 D11
João Pessoa *Town* Brazil 37 C12
Jodhpur *Town* India 77 D8
Johannesburg *Town* South Africa 69 J9
John o'Groats *Town* Scotland, UK 41 C9
Johor Baharu *Town* Malaysia 80 F2
Joliet *Town* Illinois, USA 20 G6

Jönköping *Town* Sweden 42 H7
Jordan *Country* 73
Jordan *River* Jordan 73 H9
Jorhat *Town* India 77 D12
Joseph Bonaparte Gulf 90 B7
Juazeiro *Town* Brazil 37 C11
Juazeiro do Norte *Town* Brazil 37 C11
Juba *Capital* South Sudan 67 F8
Judenburg *Town* Austria 40 G11
Juliaca *Town* Peru 36 D6
Juneau *State capital* Alaska, USA 25 C11
Jyväskylä *Town* Finland 43 F10

K2 *Mountain* China/Pakistan 77 B9
Kabul *Capital* Afghanistan 76 B7
Kabwe *Town* Zambia 69 F9
Kachchh, Rann of India 76 E7
Kaduna *Town* Nigeria 65 H10
Kagoshima *Town* Japan 82 I5
Kairouan *Town* Tunisia 62 D7
Kaiserslautern *Town* Germany 50 G7
Kalahari Desert Namibia 68 H7
Kalamata *Town* Peleponnese, Greece 49 I11
Kalamazoo *Town* Michigan, USA 20 G7
Kalemie *Town* DRC 69 E9
Kalgoorlie *Town* Australia 90 G5
Kaliningrad *Town* Russian Fed. 58 G5
Kalisz *Town* Poland 56 E7
Kamina *Town* DRC 69 E8
Kamloops *Town* British Columbia, Canada 28 H6
Kampala *Capital* Uganda 67 G8
Kampong Cham *Town* Cambodia 78 H5
Kananga *Town* DRC 69 E8
Kanazawa *Town* Japan 83 F8
Kandy *Town* Sri Lanka 77 J9
Kankan *Town* Guinea 64 H5
Kano *Town* Nigeria 65 G10
Kanpur *Town* India 77 D9
Kansas *River* Kansas, USA 27 D13
Kansas *State* USA 27
Kansas City *Town* Missouri, USA 22 B4
Kansk *Town* Russian Fed. 86 G6
Kaposvár *Town* Hungary 54 D5
Karabük *Town* Turkey 73 B8
Karachi *Town* Pakistan 76 D6
Kara Sea 17 G14, 59 B10, 86 D4
Karbala *Town* Iraq 74 C7
Kardhitsa *Town* Greece 49 G11
Karlovac *Town* Croatia 49 C8
Karlovy Vary *Town* Czech Republic 56 G4
Karlskrona *Town* Sweden 42 I7

Karlsruhe *Town* Germany 50 H7
Karlstad *Town* Sweden 42 G7
Kars *Town* Turkey 73 C13
Kasai (Cassai) *River* Angola/DRC 68 D7
Kashi *Town* China 84 E4
Kassala *Town* Sudan 67 C9
Kassel *Town* Germany 51 E9
Katherine *Town* Australia 91 B8
Kathmandu *Capital* Nepal 77 D10
Katowice *Town* Poland 57 G8
Katsina *Town* Nigeria 65 G10
Kattegat *Sea* 42 H6
Kaunas *Town* Lithuania 58 G5
Kaválla *Town* Greece 49 F12
Kawasaki *Town* Japan 83 G10
Kayseri *Town* Turkey 73 D9
Kazakhstan *Country* 86
Kazan *Town* Russian Fed. 59 F9
Kecskemét *Town* Hungary 54 D6
Kelang *Town* Malaysia 80 E2
Kemerovo *Town* Russian Fed. 86 G5
Kemi *Town* Finland 43 D9
Kénitra *Town* Morocco 62 D3
Kentucky *State* USA 23
Kenya *Country* 67
Kerman *Town* Iran 75 D10
Kesennuma *Town* Japan 83 E10
Kettering *Town* Ohio, USA 21 H8
Key West *Town* Florida, USA 23 J11
Khabarovsk *Town* Russian Fed. 87 H9
Kharkiv *Town* Ukraine 58 H7
Khartoum *Capital* Sudan 67 C8
Khaskovo *Town* Bulgaria I11
Khon Kaen *Town* Thailand 78 G4
Khulna *Town* Bangladesh 77 F11
Kiel *Town* Germany 51 B10
Kiev *Capital* Ukraine 58 G6
Kigali *Capital* Rwanda 66 G7
Kigoma *Town* Tanzania 66 H7
Kikwit *Town* DRC 68 D7
Kilimanjaro, Mount Tanzania 67 H9
Kimberley *Town* South Africa 69 I8
Kimberley Plateau Australia 90 C6
Kingston *Capital* Jamaica 35 D8
Kingstown *Capital* St. Vincent 35 E12
Kinshasa *Capital* DRC 68 D6
Kiribati *Country* 93 I13
Kirikkale *Town* Turkey 73 C9
Kirkuk *Town* Iraq 74 B7
Kirov *Town* Russian Fed. 58 G6
Kiruna *Town* Sweden 43 C8
Kisangani *Town* DRC 69 C8
Kismaayo *Town* Somalia 67 G10
Kisumu *Town* Kenya 67 G8
Kitakyushu *Town* Japan 82 H5
Kitchener *Town* Ontario, Canada 29 J11

Kitwe *Town* Zambia 69 F9
Kivu, Lake DRC/Rwanda 66 H7, 69 D9
Klagenfurt *Town* Austria 40 H11
Klamath Falls *Town* Oregon, USA 24 G3
Knoxville *Town* Tennessee, USA 23 C9
Kobe *Town* Japan 82 H7
Koblenz *Town* Germany 50 F7
Kochi (Cochin) *Town* India 77 I8
Kochi *Town* Japan 82 H7
Kodiak *Town* Alaska, USA 25 C10
Kofu *Town* Japan 83 G9
Kokshetau *Town* Kazakhstan 86 H3
Kolhapur *Town* India 76 G7
Kolkata (Calcutta) *Town* India 77 F11
Kolwezi *Town* DRC 69 E8
Komatsu *Town* Japan 83 F8
Komsomol'sk-na-Amure *Town* Russian Fed. 87 H9
Konya *Town* Turkey 73 E8
Koper *Town* Slovenia 48 B7
Korçë *Town* Albania 49 F10
Korea, North *Country* 85
Korea, South *Country* 85
Korea Strait Japan/South Korea 82 H4, 85 E13
Koriyama *Town* Japan 83 F10
Korla *Town* China 84 E6
Kortrijk *Town* Belgium 50 E4
Kosice *Town* Slovakia 57 I10
Kosovo *Country* 49
Kosovska Mitrovica *Town* Serbia 49 D10
Koszalin *Town* Poland 56 B6
Kotka *Town* Finland 43 G10
Kotte *Capital* Sri Lanka 77 J9
Kotto *River* CAR 68 B7
Kozáni *Town* Greece 49 F11
Kozhikode (Calicut) *Town* India 77 H8
Kragujevac *Town* Serbia 49 D10
Kraków *Town* Poland 57 G9
Krasnodar *Town* Russian Fed. 58 I7
Krasnoyarsk *Town* Russian Fed. 86 G5
Krefeld *Town* Germany 50 E7
Kristiansand *Town* Norway 42 H5
Krusevac *Town* Serbia 49 D11
Kryvyy Rih *Town* Ukraine 58 H6
Kuala Lumpur *Capital* Malaysia 80 E2
Kuala Terengganu *Town* Malaysia 80 E2
Kuching *Town* Malaysia 80 F4
Kugluktuk *Town* Nunavut, Canada 28 E7
Kumamoto *Town* Japan 82 I5

Kumanovo *Town* Macedonia 49 E11
Kumasi *Town* Ghana 64 I7
Kunlun Shan *Mountain range* China 84 F6
Kunming *Town* China 85 I9
Kuopio *Town* Finland 43 E10
Kupang *Town* Indonesia 80 H7
Kure *Town* Japan 82 H6
Kushiro *Town* Japan 83 B11
Kütahya *Town* Turkey 72 D7
Kuwait *Country* 75
Kuwait City *Capital* Kuwait 75 D8
Kwangju *Town* South Korea 85 E13
Kwango *River* DRC 68 E6
Kwilu *River* DRC 68 D7
Kyoto *Town* Japan 83 G8
Kyrgyzstan *Country* 86
Kyushu *Island* Japan 82 I5
Kyustendil *Town* Bulgaria 55 I9

Labrador Sea 29 F12
La Ceiba *Town* Honduras 34 D5
La Coruña *Town* Spain 44 B5
La Crosse *Town* Wisconsin, USA 20 F4
Ladoga, Lake Russian Fed. 58 E6
Lafayette *Town* Louisiana, USA 22 H5
Lagos *Town* Nigeria 65 I8
Lagos *Town* Portugal 44 H5
Lahore *Town* Pakistan 77 C8
Lahti *Town* Finland 43 F10
Lake Charles *Town* Louisiana, USA 22 H5
Lakewood *Town* Colorado, USA 27 D10
Lalitpur *Town* India 77 E9
Lamía *Town* Greece 49 G11
Lansing *State capital* Michigan, USA 20 F7
Lanzhou *Town* China 85 F9
Laoag *Town* Philippines 79 D10
Laos *Country* 78
La Paz *Capital* Bolivia 36 D7
La Paz *Town* Mexico 30 F5
La Plata *Town* Argentina 37 G8
Laptev Sea 17 D13, 87 D8
Laredo *Town* Texas, USA 27 I12
Larissa *Town* Greece 49 G11
Larkana *Town* Pakistan 76 C7
La Rochelle *Town* France 46 E6
La Romana *Town* Dominican Republic 35 D10
Las Cruces *Town* New Mexico, USA 27 G9
La Serena *Town* Chile 36 F6
La Spezia *Town* Italy 48 C5
Las Vegas *Town* Nevada, USA 26 E6
Latina *Town* Italy 48 E6

Latvia *Country* 58
Launceston *Town* Australia 91 J11
Lausanne *Town* Switzerland 52 G1
Laval *Town* France 46 C7
Lawton *Town* Oklahoma, USA 27 F12
Lebanon *Country* 73
Lecce *Town* Italy 49 F9
Leeds *Town* England, UK 41 F9
Leeuwarden *Town* Netherlands 50 C7
Legnica *Town* Poland 56 F6
Le Havre *Town* France 47 B8
Leicester *Town* England, UK 41 G9
Leiden *Town* Netherlands 50 D6
Leipzig *Town* Germany 51 F11
Le Mans *Town* France 47 C8
Lena *River* Russian Fed. 86 G7
León *Town* Mexico 31 G8
León *Town* Nicaragua 34 E5
León *Town* Spain 44 C7
Lerwick *Town* Scotland, UK 41 A9
Leskovac *Town* Serbia 49 D11
Lesotho *Country* 69
Lethbridge *Town* Alberta, Canada 28 I7
Leuven *Town* Belgium 50 E5
Lewis *Island* Scotland, UK 40 C7
Lewiston *Town* Idaho, USA 24 E5
Lewiston *Town* Maine, USA 21 D13
Lexington *Town* Kentucky, USA 23 B8
Lhasa *Town* China 84 H7
Lianyungang *Town* China 85 F12
Liberec *Town* Czech Republic 56 F5
Liberia *Country* 64
Libreville *Capital* Gabon 68 C5
Libya *Country* 63
Libyan Desert Egypt/Libya/Sudan 63 G11, 66 A6
Liechtenstein *Country* 52
Liège *Town* Belgium 50 F6
Liepaja *Town* Latvia 58 F5
Likasi *Town* DRC 69 F8
Lille *Town* France 47 A10
Lillehammer *Town* Norway 42 F6
Lilongwe *Capital* Malawi 69 F10
Lima *Capital* Peru 36 D5
Limassol *Town* Cyprus 73 G8
Limerick *Town* Republic of Ireland 40 G6
Limoges *Town* France 47 E8
Limón *Town* Costa Rica 34 F6
Limpopo *River* South Africa 69 H9
Linares *Town* Spain 45 G9
Lincoln *State capital* Nebraska, USA 25 I14
Lincoln Sea 17 G11
Lindi *Town* Tanzania 67 J10

Linköping *Town* Sweden 42 H7
Linz *Town* Austria 40 E11
Lipetsk *Town* Russian Fed. 58 G7
Lisbon *Capital* Portugal 44 G4
Lithuania *Country* 58
Little Rock *State capital* Arkansas, USA 22 E5
Liuzhou *Town* China 85 I10
Liverpool *Town* England, UK 41 G8
Livingstone *Town* Zambia 69 G8
Livorno *Town* Italy 48 D5
Ljubljana *Capital* Slovenia 48 B7
Lleida *Town* Spain 45 C11
Lobamba *Capital* Swaziland 69 I9
Lobito *Town* Angola 68 F6
Lodz *Town* Poland 57 E8
Logroño *Town* Spain 45 C9
Loire *River* France 46 D7
Lomami *River* DRC 69 D8
Lomas de Zamora *Town* Argentina 37 G8
Lomé *Capital* Togo 65 I8
London *Capital* England, UK 41 H10
London *Town* Ontario, Canada 29 J11
Londonderry *Town* Northern Ireland, UK 40 E7
Long Beach *Town* California, USA 26 F5
Long Island New York, USA 21 F12
Longview *Town* Texas, USA 27 G14
Lorca *Town* Spain 45 H10
Lorient *Town* France 46 C6
Los Angeles *Town* California, USA 26 F5
Los Angeles *Town* Chile 36 H6
Los Mochis *Town* Mexico 30 E6
Louisiana *State* USA 22
Louisville *Town* Kentucky, USA 23 B8
Lowell *Town* Massachusetts, USA 21 E13
Lower Hutt *Town* New Zealand 93 F9
Luanda *Capital* Angola 68 E6
Lubango *Town* Angola 68 F6
Lubbock *Town* Texas, USA 27 F11
Lübeck *Town* Germany 51 B10
Lublin *Town* Poland 57 F11
Lubumbashi *Town* DRC 69 F9
Lucknow *Town* India 77 D9
Lüderitz *Town* Namibia 68 I6
Ludhiana *Town* India 77 C8
Ludwigshafen *Town* Germany 51 G7
Luena *Town* Angola 68 F7
Lugano *Town* Switzerland 52 H4
Lugo *Town* Spain 44 B6
Luleå *Town* Sweden 43 D9

Lund *Town* Sweden 42 I7
Lüneburg *Town* Germany 51 C10
Luoyang *Town* China 85 F10
Lusaka *Capital* Zambia 69 F9
Luxembourg *Capital* Luxembourg 50 G6
Luxembourg *Country* 50 G6
Luxor *Town* Egypt 63 G13
Luzon *Island* Philippines 79 E10
Lviv *Town* Ukraine 58 H5
Lynchburg *Town* Virgina, USA 23 B11
Lyon *Town* France 47 F10

Maas (Meuse) *River* Belgium/ France/Netherlands 50 E6
Maastricht *Town* Netherlands 50 E6
Macapá *Town* Brazil 37 B9
Macau *Town* China 85 I11
Macdonnell Ranges Australia 91 E8
Macedonia *Country* 49
Maceio *Town* Brazil 37 C11
Mackay *Town* Australia 91 D12
Macon *Town* Georgia, USA 23 E9
Ma'daba *Town* Jordan 73 I10
Madagascar *Country* 69
Madeira *River* Brazil 37 B8
Madison *State capital* Wisconsin, USA 20 F5
Madras *See* Chennai
Madrid *Capital* Spain 45 E8
Madurai *Town* India 77 I8
Magadan *Town* Russian Fed. 87 G11
Magdeburg *Town* Germany 51 D10
Magnitogorsk *Town* Russian Fed. 59 G10
Mahajanga *Town* Madagascar 69 G12
Maiduguri *Town* Nigeria 65 H11
Main *River* Germany 51 G10
Maine, Gulf of 21 D14
Maine *State* USA 21
Mainz *Town* Germany 51 G8
Maitri (India) *RS* Antarctica 16 C5
Malabo *Capital* Equatorial Guinea 68 C5
Málaga *Town* Spain 45 I8
Malakal *Town* Sudan 67 D8
Malang *Town* Indonesia 80 H4
Malatya *Town* Turkey 73 D11
Malawi *Country* 69
Malaysia *Country* 80
Mali *Country* 64
Mallorca Balearic Islands, Spain 45 E13
Malmö *Town* Sweden 42 I7
Malta *Country* 48
Manado *Town* Indonesia 80 F7
Managua *Capital* Nicaragua 34 E5
Manama *Capital* Bahrain 75 E8

Manaus *Town* Brazil 37 B8

Manchester *Town* England, UK 41 G9

Manchester *Town* New Hampshire, USA 21 E13

Mandalay *Town* Burma (Myanmar) 78 E2

Mangalore *Town* India 76 H7

Manila *Capital* Philippines 79 F10

Manisa *Town* Turkey 72 D5

Manitoba *Province* Canada 29

Manizales *Town* Colombia 35 H8

Mankato *Town* Minnesota, USA 20 F3

Mannheim *Town* Germany 51 G8

Manta *Town* Ecuador 36 B5

Maputo *Capital* Mozambique 69 I9

Marabá *Town* Brazil 37 B9

Maracaibo *Town* Venezuela 35 F9

Maradi *Town* Niger 65 G10

Marajo Island Brazil 37 B9

Marambio (Argentina) *RS* Antarctica 16 D1

Marbella *Town* Spain 45 I8

Mardan *Town* Pakistan 77 B8

Mar del Plata *Town* Argentina 37 G8

Maribor *Town* Slovenia 49 B8

Marie Byrd Land Antarctica 16 F3

Marka *Town* Somalia 67 G11

Marmara, Sea of 72 C6

Marquette *Town* Michigan, USA 20 D5

Marrakech *Town* Morocco 62 E2

Marseille *Town* France 47 H10

Marshall Islands *Country* 93 H12

Martin *Town* Slovakia 57 H8

Martinique *Dep. territory* France 35 E12

Maryland *State* USA 21

Masaka *Town* Uganda 67 G8

Maseru *Capital* Lesotho 69 I8

Mashhad *Town* Iran 75 B11

Massa *Town* Italy 48 C5

Massachusetts *State* USA 21

Massawa *Town* Eritrea 67 C9

Massif Central France 47 F9

Matadi *Town* DRC 68 D6

Matamoros *Town* Mexico 31 E10

Mataram *Town* Indonesia 80 H5

Mataró *Town* Spain 45 C13

Matsue *Town* Japan 82 G6

Matsumoto *Town* Japan 83 G9

Matsuyama *Town* Japan 82 H6

Matterhorn, Mount Switzerland 52 H2

Maun *Town* Botswana 69 G8

Mauritania *Country* 64

Mauritius *Country* 69

Mawson (Australia) *RS* Antarctica 16 E6

Mayotte *Dep. territory* France 69 F12

Mazar-e Sharif *Town* Afghanistan 76 A7

Mazatlán *Town* Mexico 30 F7

Mbabane *Capital* Swaziland 69 I9

Mbandaka *Town* DRC 68 C7

Mbeya *Town* Tanzania 67 I9

Mbuji-Mayi *Town* DRC 69 E8

McKinley, Mount Alaska, USA 25 B11

McMurdo (US) *RS* Antarctica 16 H5

Mecca *Town* Saudi Arabia 74 G5

Mechelen *Town* Belgium 50 E5

Medan *Town* Indonesia 80 E1

Medellín *Town* Colombia 35 G8

Medicine Hat *Town* Alberta, Canada 28 I7

Medina *Town* Saudi Arabia 74 F5

Mediterranean Sea 45, 47, 62, 73

Meerut *Town* India 77 D9

Mekong *River* Asia 78 G5, 85 I9

Melbourne *Town* Australia 91 I11

Melilla *Town* Spain 45 J9, 62 D4

Melville Island Canada 17 E9

Memphis *Town* Tennessee, USA 22 D6

Mendoza *Town* Argentina 36 G7

Menorca Balearic Islands, Spain 45 E14

Mérida *Town* Mexico 31 G13, 44 F7

Mérida *Town* Spain 44 F7

Mesa *Town* Arizona, USA 26 F7

Messina *Town* Sicily, Italy 48 H7

Metairie *Town* Louisiana, USA 22 H6

Metz *Town* France 47 C11

Meuse (Maas) *River* Belgium/ France/Netherlands 50 F5

Mexicali *Town* Mexico 30 B4

Mexico, Gulf of 23 H8, 27 J14, 31 F11

Mexico *Country* 30

Mexico City *Capital* Mexico 31 H9

Miami *Town* Florida, USA 23 I12

Michigan, Lake USA 20 E6

Michigan *State* USA 20

Micronesia *Country* 93 H11

Middlesbrough *Town* England, UK 41 F9

Midland *Town* Texas, USA 27 G11

Milan *Town* Italy 48 B5

Miles City *Town* Montana, USA 25 F10

Milwaukee *Town* Wisconsin, USA 20 F6

Mindanao *Island* Philippines 79 G12

Mindoro Strait South China Sea 79 G10

Minneapolis *Town* Minnesota, USA 20 E3

Minnesota *State* USA 20

Minot *Town* N Dakota, USA 25 E12

Minsk *Capital* Belarus 58 G6

Mirny (Russian Federation) *RS* Antarctica 16 F7

Mirpur Khas *Town* Pakistan 76 D7

Miskolc *Town* Hungary 54 B7

Mississippi *River* USA 20 F4, 22 E6

Mississippi *State* USA 22

Missouri *River* Montana, USA 25 E10

Missouri *State* USA 22

Mito *Town* Japan 83 F10

Miyako *Town* Japan 83 D10

Miyakonojo *Town* Japan 82 I5

Miyazaki *Town* Japan 82 I6

Mobile *Town* Alabama, USA 22 G7

Modesto *Town* California, USA 26 C4

Mogadishu *Capital* Somalia 67 F11

Moldova *Country* 58

Molucca Sea 80 F7

Mombasa *Town* Kenya 67 H10

Monaco *Capital* Monaco 47 H11

Monaco *Country* 47

Monclova *Town* Mexico 31 E9

Mongolia *Country* 85

Monroe *Town* Louisiana, USA 22 F5

Monrovia *Capital* Liberia 64 I4

Mons *Town* Belgium 50 F5

Montana *State* USA 25

Montana *Town* Bulgaria 55 H9

Montauban *Town* France 46 G7

Mont Blanc *Mountain* France 47 F11

Mont-de-Marsan *Town* France 46 F7

Montego Bay *Town* Jamaica 35 C8

Montélimar *Town* France 47 G10

Montenegro *Country* 49

Monterey *Town* California, USA 26 D4

Montería *Town* Colombia 35 F8

Monterrey *Town* Mexico 31 E9

Montevideo *Capital* Uruguay 37 G8

Montgomery *State capital* Alabama, USA 23 F8

Montluçon *Town* France 47 E9

Montpelier *State capital* Vermont, USA 21 D12

Montpellier *Town* France 47 H9

Montreal *Town* Quebec, Canada 29 I12

Montserrat *Dep. territory* UK 35 D12

Monza *Town* Italy 48 B5

Moorhead *Town* Minnesota, USA 20 D2

Mopti *Town* Mali 64 G6

Morelia *Town* Mexico 31 H8

Morocco *Country* 62

Moroni *Capital* Comoros 69 F12

Moscow *Capital* Russian Fed. 58 F7

Mosselbaai *Town* South Africa 68 J7

Mossoró *Town* Brazil 37 B11

Mostar *Town* Bosnia and Herz. 49 D9

Mosul *Town* Iraq 74 B6

Moulmein *Town* Burma (Myanmar) 78 G3

Moundou *Town* Chad 65 I12

Mount Isa *Town* Australia 91 D10

Mozambique *Country* 69

Mufulira *Town* Zambia 69 F9

Mulhouse *Town* France 47 D12

Multan *Town* Pakistan 77 C8

Mumbai (Bombay) *Town* India 76 F7

Muncie *Town* Indiana, USA 20 H7

Munich *Town* Germany 51 I10

Münster *Town* Germany 50 D7

Murcia *Town* Spain 45 G10

Murmansk *Town* Russian Fed. 58 C7

Muroran *Town* Japan 83 C10

Murray *River* Australia 91 H11

Muscat *Capital* Oman 75 F11

Mwanza *Town* Tanzania 67 H8

Mweru, Lake DRC 69 E9

Myanmar *See* Burma

Myrtle Beach *Town* S Carolina, USA 23 D11

Mysore *Town* India 77 H8

Myvatn *Lake* Iceland 43 H13

Nacala *Town* Mozambique 69 F11

Nagano *Town* Japan 83 F9

Nagaoka *Town* Japan 83 F9

Nagasaki *Town* Japan 82 I5

Nagoya *Town* Japan 83 G8

Nagpur *Town* India 77 F9

Nain *Town* Newfoundland and Labrador, Canada 29 G12

Nairobi *Capital* Kenya 67 G9

Nakhon Ratchasima *Town* Thailand 78 G4

Nakhon Sawan *Town* Thailand 78 G4

Nakhon Si Thammarat *Town* Thailand 78 I4

Nakuru *Town* Kenya 67 G9

Nam Dinh *Town* Vietnam 78 E5

Namib Desert Namibia 68 H6

Namibe *Town* Angola 68 F6

Namibia *Country* 68

Nampula *Town* Mozambique 69 F11

Namur *Town* Belgium 50 F5

Nanchang *Town* China 85 G11

Nanchong *Town* China 85 G9
Nancy *Town* France 47 C11
Nanjing *Town* China 85 F12
Nanning *Town* China 85 I10
Nantes *Town* France 46 D6
Napier *Town* New Zealand 93 D10
Naples *Town* Italy 48 F7
Narvik *Town* Norway 43 C8
Nashville *State capital* Tennessee, USA 23 C8
Nassau *Capital* Bahamas 35 A8
Nasser, Lake Egypt 63 H13
Natal *Town* Brazil 37 C12
Nauru *Country* 93 H12
Naypyidaw *Capital* Burma (Myanmar) 78 F2
Nazareth *Town* Israel 73 H9
Nazilli *Town* Turkey 72 D6
Nazret *Town* Ethiopia 67 E10
N'Djamena *Capital* Chad 65 H12
Ndola *Town* Zambia 69 F9
Neápolis *Town* Greece 49 I11
Near Islands Alaska, USA 25 B8
Nebraska *State* USA 25
Negev Desert Israel 73 I9
Negotin *Town* Serbia 49 C11
Negro *River* Brazil 36 B7
Nellore *Town* India 77 H9
Nelson *Town* New Zealand 93 F8
Nepal *Country* 77
Netanya *Town* Israel 73 H9
Netherlands *Country* 50
Neubrandenburg *Town* Germany 51 C11
Neuchâtel *Town* Switzerland 52 F2
Neumayer III (Germany) *RS* Antarctica 16 C4
Neuquén *Town* Argentina 36 H7
Nevada *State* USA 26
Newark *Town* New Jersey, USA 21 F12
New Brunswick *Province* Canada 29
New Caledonia *Dep. territory* France 93 J12
Newcastle *Town* Australia 91 G12
Newcastle upon Tyne *Town* England, UK 41 E9
New Delhi *Capital* India 77 D9
Newfoundland and Labrador *Province* Canada 29
New Guinea *Island* Indonesia 81 G10
New Hampshire *State* USA 21
New Haven *Town* Connecticut, USA 21 F12
New Jersey *State* USA 21
New Mexico *State* USA 27
New Orleans *Town* Louisiana, USA 22 H6

New Plymouth *Town* New Zealand 93 D9
Newport *Town* Vermont, USA 21 C12
Newport *Town* Wales, UK 41 H8
Newport News *Town* Virginia, USA 23 B12
New South Wales *State* Australia 91
New York *State* USA 21
New York City *Town* New York, USA 21 F12
New Zealand *Country* 92
Nha Trang *Town* Vietnam 78 H7
Niagara Falls USA 21 F9
Niamey *Capital* Niger 65 G8
Nicaragua *Country* 34
Nice *Town* France 47 H11
Nicobar Islands India 77 J12
Nicosia *Capital* Cyprus 73 F8
Niger *Country* 65
Niger *River* West Africa 65 I9
Nigeria *Country* 65
Niigata *Town* Japan 83 F9
Niksic *Town* Montenegro 49 D9
Nile *River* East Africa 63 F13, 66 B7
Nîmes *Town* France 47 G9
Ningbo *Town* China 85 G12
Nis *Town* Serbia 49 D11
Nitra *Town* Slovakia 57 I8
Niue *Dep. territory* New Zealand 93 I13
Nizhnevartovsk *Town* Russian Fed. 86 G4
Nizhniy Novgorod *Town* Russian Fed. 59 F8
Nobeoka *Town* Japan 82 I6
Norfolk *Town* Nebraska, USA 25 H13
Norfolk *Town* Virginia, USA 23 B12
Noril'sk *Town* Russian Fed. 86 E5
Norman *Town* Oklahoma, USA 27 F13
Norrköping *Town* Sweden 43 H8
Northampton *Town* England, UK 41 H9
North Cape New Zealand 93 A8
North Cape Norway 43 A9
North Carolina *State* USA 23
North Dakota *State* USA 25
Northern Ireland *Country* UK 40
Northern Mariana Islands *Dep. territory* USA 93 G11
Northern Territory *State* Australia 91
North Island New Zealand 93
North Korea *See* Korea, North
North Sea 41, 42, 50
Northwest Territories *Province* Canada 28

Norway *Country* 42
Norwegian Sea 17 I11, 43 J13
Norwich *Town* England, UK 41 G10
Nottingham *Town* England, UK 41 G9
Nouadhibou *Town* Mauritania 64 D3
Nouakchott *Capital* Mauritania 64 E3
Nova Iguaçu *Town* Brazil 37 E10
Novara *Town* Italy 48 B4
Nova Scotia *Province* Canada 29
Novaya Zemlya *Island* Russian Fed. 17 G13, 59 B10
Novgorod *Town* Russian Fed. 58 F6
Novi Sad *Town* Serbia 49 C10
Novokuznetsk *Town* Russian Fed. 86 H5
Novosibirsk *Town* Russian Fed. 86 H5
Nubian Desert Sudan 67 A8
Nueva Gerona *Town* Cuba 34 B6
Nuevo Laredo *Town* Mexico 31 D9
Nunavut *Province* Canada 29
Nuremberg *Town* Germany 51 H10
Nyala *Town* Sudan 66 D6
Nyíregyháza *Town* Hungary 55 C8

Oakland *Town* California, USA 26 C4
Oamaru *Town* New Zealand 92 I7
Oaxaca *Town* Mexico 31 I10
Ob *River* Russian Fed. 86 G4
Obihiro *Town* Japan 83 B11
Oceanside *Town* California, USA 26 F5
Odense *Town* Denmark 42 I6
Oder *River* Poland 56 F7
Odessa *Town* Texas, USA 27 G11
Odessa *Town* Ukraine 58 H6
Offenbach *Town* Germany 51 G8
Ogaden Plateau Ethiopia 67 E11
Ogbomosho *Town* Nigeria 65 I9
Ogden *Town* Utah, USA 27 C8
Ohio *State* USA 21
Ohrid, Lake Albania/Macedonia 49 F10
Oita *Town* Japan 82 H6
Okavango Delta Botswana 68 G7
Okayama *Town* Japan 82 H7
Okeechobee, Lake Florida, USA 23 I11
Okhotsk, Sea of 87 G10
Oklahoma *State* USA 27
Oklahoma City *State capital* Oklahoma, USA 27 F13
Öland *Island* Sweden 43 I8
Oldenburg *Town* Germany 51 C8
Olomouc *Town* Czech Republic 56 H7

Olsztyn *Town* Poland 57 C9
Olympia *State capital* Washington, USA 24 D3
Olympus, Mount Greece 49 F11
Omaha *Town* Nebraska, USA 25 I14
Oman, Gulf of 75 F11
Oman *Country* 75
Omdurman *Town* Sudan 67 C8
Omsk *Town* Russian Fed. 86 H4
Onega, Lake Russian Fed. 58 E7
Onega *Town* Russian Fed. 58 D7
Onitsha *Town* Nigeria 65 I9
Ontario, Lake USA 21 E10
Ontario *Province* Canada 29
Opole *Town* Poland 56 F7
Oradea *Town* Romania 55 C8
Oran *Town* Algeria 62 D5
Orange *River* South Africa 69 I8
Orcadas (Argentina) *RS* Antarctica 16 C1
Ordu *Town* Turkey 73 C11
Örebro *Town* Sweden 42 G7
Oregon *State* USA 24
Orenburg *Town* Russian Fed. 59 G10, 86 H2
Orense *Town* Spain 44 C6
Orkney Islands Scotland, UK 41 B9
Orlando *Town* Florida, USA 23 H11
Orléans *Town* France 47 D8
Örnsköldsvik *Town* Sweden 43 E8
Orsk *Town* Russian Fed. 59 G10
Oruro *Town* Bolivia 36 D7
Osaka *Town* Japan 83 H8
Oshawa *Town* Ontario, Canada 29 J11
Oshkosh *Town* Wisconsin, USA 20 F5
Osijek *Town* Croatia 49 B9
Oslo *Capital* Norway 42 G6
Osmaniye *Town* Turkey 73 E10
Osnabrück *Town* Germany 51 D8
Osorno *Town* Chile 36 H6
Ostend *Town* Belgium 50 E4
Östersund *Town* Sweden 42 E7
Ostrava *Town* Czech Republic 57 H8
Otago Peninsula New Zealand 92 I7
Otaru *Town* Japan 83 B10
Ottawa *Capital* Canada 29 I12
Ouagadougou *Capital* Burkina Faso 64 G7
Oujda *Town* Morocco 62 D4
Oulu *Town* Finland 43 D10
Outer Hebrides *Island group* Scotland, UK 40 C7
Oviedo *Town* Spain 44 B7
Owensboro *Town* Kentucky, USA 22 B7
Oxford *Town* England, UK 41 H9
Oxnard *Town* California, USA 26 E5

Pachuca *Town* Mexico 31 G9

Pacific Ocean 24, 25, 26, 28, 30, 36, 79, 83, 85, 87, 91, 93

Padang *Town* Indonesia 80 F2

Paderborn *Town* Germany 51 E8

Paducah *Town* Kentucky, USA 22 C7

Pakistan *Country* 76

Pakxe *Town* Laos 78 G5

Palau *Country* 93 H10

Palawan Passage South China Sea 79 H9

Palembang *Town* Indonesia 80 G3

Palencia *Town* Spain 45 C8

Palermo *Town* Sicily, Italy 48 H6

Palma *Town* Mallorca, Spain 45 E13

Palmer (US) *RS* Antarctica 16 D1

Palmerston North *Town* New Zealand 93 E9

Palo Alto *Town* California, USA 26 D4

Palu *Town* Indonesia 80 F6

Pamplona *Town* Spain 45 B10

Panama, Gulf of 34 G7

Panama *Country* 34

Panama Canal Panama 34 F6

Panama City *Capital* Panama 34 F7

Pancevo *Town* Serbia 49 C10

Papua New Guinea *Country* 93

Paraguay *Country* 37

Paramaribo *Capital* Suriname 35 G13

Pardubice *Town* Czech Republic 56 G6

Paris *Capital* France 47 C9

Parma *Town* Italy 48 C5

Parnaíba *Town* Brazil 37 B11

Pasadena *Town* California, USA 26 F5

Pasadena *Town* Texas, USA 27 H14

Pasco *Town* Washington, USA 24 E5

Passau *Town* Germany 51 I11

Pasto *Town* Colombia 34 I7

Patagonia Argentina 36 I7

Paterson *Town* New Jersey, USA 21 F12

Patna *Town* India 77 E10

Pátrai *Town* Greece 49 H11

Pau *Town* France 46 G6

Pavlodar *Town* Kazakhstan 86 H4

Pearl *River* Mississippi, USA 22 G6

Pejë *Town* Kosovo 49 E10

Pechora *River* Russian Fed. 59 D9

Pécs *Town* Hungary 54 E5

Pedro Juan Caballero *Town* Paraguay 37 E8

Pegu *Town* Burma (Myanmar) 78 G2

Pekanbaru *Town* Indonesia 80 F2

Pennines *Hills* England, UK 41 F9

Pennsylvania *State* USA 21

Penza *Town* Russian Fed. 59 G8

Peoria *Town* Illinois, USA 20 H5

Pereira *Town* Colombia 35 H8

Perm *Town* Russian Fed. 59 F9

Pernik *Town* Bulgaria 55 I9

Persian Gulf 75 E8

Perth *Town* Australia 90 G4

Perth *Town* Scotland, UK 41 D8

Peru *Country* 36

Perugia *Town* Italy 48 D6

Pescara *Town* Italy 48 E7

Peshawar *Town* Pakistan 77 B8

Peterborough *Town* England, UK 41 G10

Petropavlovsk-Kamchatskiy *Town* Russian Fed. 87 H11

Petrozavodsk *Town* Russian Fed. 58 E7

Pforzheim *Town* Germany 51 H8

Philadelphia *Town* Pennsylvania, USA 21 G12

Philippines *Country* 79

Phnom Penh *Capital* Cambodia 78 H5

Phoenix *State capital* Arizona, USA 26 F7

Phuket *Town* Thailand 78 I3

Piacenza *Town* Italy 48 C5

Pierre *State capital* S Dakota, USA 25 G12

Pietermaritzburg *Town* South Africa 69 I9

Pietersburg *Town* South Africa 69 H9

Pinar del Río *Town* Cuba 34 B6

Pine Bluff *Town* Arkansas, USA 22 E5

Piraeus *Town* Greece 49 H12

Pisa *Town* Italy 48 D5

Pistoia *Town* Italy 48 C6

Pitesti *Town* Romania 55 F10

Pittsburgh *Town* Pennsylvania, USA 21 G9

Piura *Town* Peru 36 B5

Plano *Town* Texas, USA 27 G13

Platte *River* Nebraska, USA 25 I12

Plauen *Town* Germany 51 F10

Plenty, Bay of New Zealand 93 C10

Pleven *Town* Bulgaria 55 H10

Plock *Town* Poland 57 D9

Ploiesti *Town* Romania 55 F11

Plovdiv *Town* Bulgaria 55 I10

Plymouth *Town* England, UK 41 I8

Plzen *Town* Czech Republic 56 G4

Podgorica *Capital* Montenegro 49 E9

Pointe-Noire *Town* Republic of the Congo 68 D5

Poitiers *Town* France 46 D7

Poland *Country* 56

Pontianak *Town* Indonesia 80 F4

Poona *See Pune*

Popayán *Town* Colombia 34 H7

Pori *Town* Finland 43 F9

Port Arthur *Town* Texas, USA 27 H14

Port Augusta *Town* Australia 91 G9

Port-au-Prince *Capital* Haiti 35 D9

Port Elizabeth *Town* South Africa 69 J8

Port-Gentil *Town* Gabon 68 C5

Port Harcourt *Town* Nigeria 65 J9

Portland *Town* Maine, USA 21 D13

Portland *Town* Oregon, USA 24 E3

Port Louis *Capital* Mauritius 69 H14

Port Macquarie *Town* Australia 91 G13

Porto *Town* Portugal 44 D5

Porto Alegre *Town* Brazil 37 F9

Port-of-Spain *Capital* Trinidad and Tobago 35 F12

Porto-Novo *Capital* Benin 65 I8

Porto Velho *Town* Brazil 36 C7

Portoviejo *Town* Ecuador 36 B5

Port Said *Town* Egypt 63 E13

Portsmouth *Town* England, UK 41 I9

Portsmouth *Town* New Hampshire, USA 21 D13

Portsmouth *Town* Virginia, USA 23 B12

Port Sudan *Town* Sudan 67 B9

Portugal *Country* 44

Potosí *Town* Bolivia 36 E7

Potsdam *Town* Germany 51 D11

Poznan *Town* Poland 56 E7

Prague *Capital* Czech Republic 56 G5

Praia *Capital* Cape Verde 64 F1

Prato *Town* Italy 48 D6

Presidente Eduardo Frei (Chile) *RS* Antarctica 16 D1

Presov *Town* Slovakia 57 H10

Prespa, Lake Macedonia 49 F10

Presque Isle *Town* Maine, USA 21 B13

Pretoria *Capital* South Africa 69 H9

Préveza *Town* Greece 49 G10

Prichard *Town* Alabama, USA 22 G7

Prilep *Town* Macedonia 49 E11

Prince Edward Island *Province* Canada 29

Prince George *Town* British Columbia, Canada 28 H6

Pristina *Capital* Kosovo 49 D10

Prizren *Town* Serbia 49 E10

Prome *Town* Burma (Myanmar) 78 F2

Providence *State capital* Rhode Island, USA 21 E13

Provo *Town* Utah, USA 27 C8

Pucallpa *Town* Peru 36 C6

Puducherry *Town* India 77 H9

Puebla *Town* Mexico 31 H10

Pueblo *Town* Colorado, USA 27 D10

Puerto Ayacucho *Town* Venezuela 35 G10

Puerto Montt *Town* Chile 36 H6

Puerto Princesa *Town* Philippines 79 G10

Puerto Rico *Dep. territory* USA 35 D11

Pula *Town* Croatia 48 C7

Pune (Poona) *Town* India 76 F7

Puno *Town* Peru 36 D6

Punta Alta *Town* Argentina 37 H8

Punta Arenas *Town* Chile 36 J7

Puntarenas *Town* Costa Rica 34 F5

Pusan *Town* South Korea 85 E13

Putrajaya *Capital* Malaysia 80 E2

Pyongyang *Capital* North Korea 85 D12

Pyrenees *Mountain range* France/ Spain 45 C11, 46 H7

Qamdo *Town* China 85 H8

Qatar *Country* 75

Qattara Depression Egypt 63 F12

Qena *Town* Egypt 63 G13

Qilian Shan *Mountain range* China 85 F8

Qingdao *Town* China 85 E12

Qom *Town* Iran 75 C8

Quebec *Province* Canada 29

Quebec *Province capital* Quebec, Canada 29 I12

Queen Elizabeth Islands Canada 17 F9

Queensland *State* Australia 91

Queenstown *Town* Australia 91 J11

Quelimane *Town* Mozambique 69 G10

Querétaro *Town* Mexico 31 G9

Quetta *Town* Pakistan 76 C7

Quezaltenango *Town* Guatemala 34 D4

Quibdó *Town* Colombia 34 G7

Quimper *Town* France 46 B5

Qui Nhon *Town* Vietnam 78 G7

Rabat *Capital* Morocco 62 D3

Radom *Town* Poland 57 F10

Ragusa *Town* Sicily, Italy 48 H7

Rainier, Mount Washington, USA 24 D4

Raipur *Town* India 77 F9

Rajshahi *Town* Bangladesh 77 E11

Raleigh *State capital* N Carolina, USA 23 C11

Rancagua *Town* Chile 36 G7

Randers *Town* Denmark 42 I6

Sarajevo *Capital* Bosnia and Herz. 49 D9

Saratov *Town* Russian Fed. 59 G8

Sarawak Malaysia 80 F4

Sardinia *Island* Italy 48 F4

Sarh *Town* Chad 65 H13

Sariwon *Town* North Korea 85 D12

Sasebo *Town* Japan 82 H5

Saskatchewan *Province* Canada 29

Saskatoon *Town* Saskatchewan, Canada 29 H8

Sassari *Town* Sardinia, Italy 48 F4

Satu Mare *Town* Romania 55 C8

Saudi Arabia *Country* 74

Savannah *Town* Georgia, USA 23 F11

Savona *Town* Italy 48 C4

Saynshand *Town* Mongolia 85 D10

Scheldt *River* Belgium 50 E4

Schenectady *Town* New York, USA 21 E12

Schwaz *Town* Austria 40 F8

Schwerin *Town* Germany 51 C10

Scotland *Country* UK 41

Scott Base (New Zealand) *RS* Antarctica 16 G4

Scranton *Town* Pennsylvania, USA 21 F11

Seattle *Town* Washington, USA 24 D4

Ségou *Town* Mali 64 G6

Segovia *Town* Spain 45 D8

Seine *River* France 47 B9

Sekondi-Takoradi *Town* Ghana 64 I7

Semarang *Town* Indonesia 80 H4

Sendai *Town* Japan 83 E10

Senegal *Country* 64

Senegal *River* Senegal 64 F4

Seoul *Capital* South Korea 85 E13

Serbia *Country* 49

Serov *Town* Russian Fed. 86 G3

Sète *Town* France 47 H9

Setúbal *Town* Portugal 44 G5

Sevastopol *Town* Crimea, Ukraine 58 I7

Severn *River* England, UK 41 H9

Severnaya Zemlya Russian Fed. 17 F13, 86 C6

Seville *Town* Spain 44 H7

Seychelles *Country* 69

Sfax *Town* Tunisia 62 D7

Shanghai *Town* China 85 F12

Shannon *River* Republic of Ireland 40 G6

Sheberghan *Town* Afghanistan 76 A7

Sheffield *Town* England, UK 41 G9

Shenyang *Town* China 85 D12

Sherbrooke *Town* Quebec, Canada 29 I12

's-Hertogenbosch *Town* Netherlands 50 D6

Shetland Islands Scotland, UK 41 A9

Shimonoseki *Town* Japan 82 H5

Shinyanga *Town* Tanzania 67 H8

Shiraz *Town* Iran 75 D9

Shizuoka *Town* Japan 83 G9

Shkodër *Town* Albania 49 E10

Showa (Japan) *RS* Antarctica 16 D6

Shreveport *Town* Louisiana, USA 22 F4

Shumen *Town* Bulgaria 55 H12

Sibenik *Town* Croatia 49 D8

Siberia Russian Fed. 86 F7

Sibiu *Town* Romania 55 E10

Sicily *Island* Italy 48 H7

Sidi Bel Abbès *Town* Algeria 62 D5

Siegen *Town* Germany 51 F8

Siena *Town* Italy 48 D6

Sierra de Gredos *Mountain range* Spain 44 E7

Sierra Leone *Country* 64

Sierra Nevada *Mountain range* California, USA 26 C5

Sierra Nevada *Mountain range* Spain 45 H9

Signy (UK) *RS* Antarctica 16 C1

Silver City *Town* New Mexico, USA 27 G9

Sincelejo *Town* Colombia 35 F8

Singapore *Capital* Singapore 80 F2

Singapore *Country* 80

Sinuiju *Town* North Korea 85 D12

Sioux City *Town* Iowa, USA 20 G2

Sioux Falls *Town* S Dakota, USA 25 H14

Siracusa *Town* Sicily, Italy 48 H7

Sittwe *Town* Burma (Myanmar) 78 E1

Sivas *Town* Turkey 73 D10

Skagerrak *Sea* Norway 42 H6

Skellefteå *Town* Sweden 43 D9

Skopje *Capital* Macedonia 49 E11

Slavonski Brod *Town* Croatia 49 C9

Sligo *Town* Republic of Ireland 40 F6

Sliven *Town* Bulgaria 55 H12

Slovakia *Country* 57

Slovenia *Country* 48

Smederevo *Town* Serbia 49 C10

Smolensk *Town* Russian Fed. 58 F6

Snake *River* Idaho/Oregon, USA 24 H6

Snowdon *Mountain* Wales, UK 41 G8

Socotra *Island* Yemen 75 J10

Söderhamn *Town* Sweden 43 F8

Södertälje *Town* Sweden 43 G8

Sofia *Capital* Bulgaria 55 I9

Soledad *Town* Colombia 35 F8

Solingen *Town* Germany 50 E7

Solomon Islands *Country* 93 I12

Solomon Sea 81 G13

Somalia *Country* 67

Songea *Town* Tanzania 67 J9

Songkhla *Town* Thailand 78 J4

Soria *Town* Spain 45 C9

Sorong *Town* Indonesia 81 F9

Sousse *Town* Tunisia 62 D7

South Africa *Country* 68

Southampton *Town* England, UK 41 I9

Southampton Island Nunavut, Canada 29 F10

South Australia *State* Australia 91

South Bend *Town* Indiana, USA 20 G6

South Carolina *State* USA 23

South China Sea 79 G8, 85 J12

South Dakota *State* USA 25

Southern Ocean 16, 90

South Georgia *Dep. territory* UK 37 J10

South Island New Zealand 92

South Korea *See* Korea, South

South Orkney Islands Antarctica 16 C1

South Ossetia *State* Georgia 59 I8

South Sudan *Country* 66

Soweto *Town* South Africa 69 I8

Spain *Country* 44

Spanish Town *Town* Jamaica 35 D8

Spartanburg *Town* S Carolina, USA 23 D10

Split *Town* Croatia 49 D8

Spokane *Town* Washington, USA 24 D5

Springfield *State capital* Illinois, USA 20 I5

Springfield *Town* Massachusetts, USA 21 E12

Springfield *Town* Missouri, USA 22 C4

Srebrenica *Town* Bosnia and Herz. 49 C9

Sri Lanka *Country* 77

Stamford *Town* Connecticut, USA 21 F12

Stara Zagora *Town* Bulgaria 55 I11

Stavanger *Town* Norway 42 G5

Stavropol *Town* Russian Fed. 59 I8

Stewart Island New Zealand 92 J6

Stockholm *Capital* Sweden 43 G8

Stockton *Town* California, USA 26 C4

Stockton Plateau Texas, USA 27 H10

Stoke-on-Trent *Town* England, UK 41 G9

Strasbourg *Town* France 47 D12

Stuttgart *Town* Germany 51 H8

Subotica *Town* Serbia 49 B10

Suceava *Town* Romania 55 C11

Sucre *Capital* Bolivia 36 E7

Sudan *Country* 66

Sudbury *Town* Ontario, Canada 29 I11

Suez, Gulf of 63 F13

Suez *Town* Egypt 63 F13

Sühbaatar *Town* Mongolia 85 C9

Sukkur *Town* Pakistan 76 C7

Sulu Archipelago Philippines 79 I10

Sulu Sea 79 H10

Sumatra *Island* Indonesia 80 F2

Sunderland *Town* England, UK 41 F9

Sundsvall *Town* Sweden 43 F8

Sunnyvale *Town* California, USA 26 D4

Superior, Lake USA 20 C5

Sur *Town* Oman 75 F11

Surabaya *Town* Indonesia 80 H4

Surakarta *Town* Indonesia 80 H4

Surat *Town* India 76 E7

Surgut *Town* Russian Fed. 86 G4

Suriname *Country* 35

Surt *Town* Libya 63 E9

Suwalki *Town* Poland 57 B11

Svalbard *Dep. territory* Norway 17 H12

Swansea *Town* Wales, UK 41 H8

Swaziland *Country* 69

Sweden *Country* 43

Swindon *Town* England, UK 41 H9

Switzerland *Country* 52

Sydney *Town* Australia 91 H12

Syktyvkar *Town* Russian Fed. 59 E9

Sylhet *Town* Bangladesh 77 E12

Syracuse *Town* New York, USA 21 E11

Syria *Country* 73

Syrian Desert Syria 73 G11, 74 C6

Szczecin *Town* Poland 56 C5

Szeged *Town* Hungary 54 D6

Székesfehérvár *Town* Hungary 54 D5

Szombathely *Town* Hungary 54 D4

Tabora *Town* Tanzania 67 H8

Tabriz *Town* Iran 74 B7

Tacoma *Town* Washington, USA 24 D3

Taegu *Town* South Korea 85 E13

Taejon *Town* South Korea 85 E13

Taguatinga *Town* Brazil 37 D9

Taipei *Capital* Taiwan 85 H13

Taiwan *Country* 85

Taiyuan *Town* China 85 E10

Ta'izz *Town* Yemen 74 I7

Tajikistan *Country* 86

Takasaki *Town* Japan 83 F9

Taklimakan Desert China 84 F5
Talcahuano *Town* Chile 36 G6
Taldyqorgan *Town* Kazakhstan 86 I4
Tallahassee *State capital* Florida, USA 23 G9
Tallinn *Capital* Estonia 58 E5
Tamale *Town* Ghana 64 H7
Tamanrasset *Town* Algeria 62 H6
Tampa *Town* Florida, USA 23 H10
Tampere *Town* Finland 43 F9
Tampico *Town* Mexico 31 G10
Tamworth *Town* Australia 91 G12
Tanami Desert Australia 91 D8
Tanga *Town* Tanzania 67 H9
Tanganyika, Lake DRC/Tanzania 66 I7, 69 E9
Tangier *Town* Morocco 62 D3
Tanzania *Country* 67
Taranto *Town* Italy 49 F8
Tarbes *Town* France 46 G7
Târgu Mures *Town* Romania 55 D10
Tarija *Town* Bolivia 36 E7
Tarim Basin China 84 E6
Tarnow *Town* Poland 57 G10
Tarragona *Town* Spain 45 D12
Tarsus *Town* Turkey 73 E9
Tartu *Town* Estonia 58 F6
Tartus *Town* Syria 73 G10
Tashkent *Capital* Uzbekistan 86 I3
Tasmania *State* Australia 91
Tasman Sea 91 I12, 92 F6
Tatra Mountains Slovakia 57 H9
Taupo, Lake New Zealand 93 D10
Tauranga *Town* New Zealand 93 C10
Taurus Mountains Turkey 73 E8
Tavoy *Town* Burma (Myanmar) 78 G3
Tbilisi *Capital* Georgia 59 I8
Tegucigalpa *Capital* Honduras 34 D5
Tehran *Capital* Iran 75 B9
Tehuantepec, Gulf of 31 I11
Tekirdag *Town* Turkey 72 B6
Tel Aviv *Town* Israel 73 H9
Temuco *Town* Chile 36 H6
Tennessee *River* Alabama/ Tennessee, USA 23 D8
Tennessee *State* USA 23
Tepic *Town* Mexico 30 G7
Teramo *Town* Italy 48 D7
Teresina *Town* Brazil 37 B10
Terni *Town* Italy 48 D6
Terrasa *Town* Spain 45 C12
Terre Haute *Town* Indiana, USA 20 H6
Teruel *Town* Spain 45 E10
Tete *Town* Mozambique 69 G10
Tétouan *Town* Morocco 62 D3
Texas *State* USA 27

Thailand, Gulf of 78 H4
Thailand *Country* 78
Thai Nguyen *Town* Vietnam 78 E5
Thames *River* England, UK 41 H10
Thanh Hoa *Town* Vietnam 78 E5
The Hague *Capital* Netherlands 50 D5
Thessaloníki *Town* Greece 49 F11
Thimphu *Capital* Bhutan 77 D11
Thiruvananthapuram (Trivandrum) *Town* India 77 I8
Thun *Town* Switzerland 52 G3
Thunder Bay *Town* Ontario, Canada 29 I10
Tianjin *Town* China 85 E11
Tibesti Mountains Chad 65 E13
Tibet China 84 G6
Tibet, Plateau of China 84 G7
Tigris *River* Iraq 74 C7
Tijuana *Town* Mexico 30 B3
Tilburg *Town* Netherlands 50 E6
Timaru *Town* New Zealand 92 H7
Timisoara *Town* Romania 54 E7
Tindouf *Town* Algeria 62 F2
Tiranë *Capital* Albania 49 F10
Tiraspol *Town* Moldova 58 H6
Tiruchchirappalli *Town* India 77 I8
Tisza *River* Central Europe 54 D7
Titicaca, Lake Peru 36 D6
Tocantins *River* Brazil 37 C10
Togo *Country* 65
Tokelau *Dep. territory* New Zealand 93 I13
Tokushima *Town* Japan 82 H7
Tokyo *Capital* Japan 83 G10
Toledo *Town* Ohio, USA 21 G8
Toledo *Town* Spain 45 E8
Toluca *Town* Mexico 31 H9
Tolyatti *Town* Russian Fed. 59 G9
Tomakomai *Town* Japan 83 C10
Tombouctou *Town* Mali 64 F7
Tomsk *Town* Russian Fed. 86 G5
Tonga *Country* 93 I13
Tonkin, Gulf of 78 E5, 85 J10
Tonopah *Town* Nevada, USA 26 D6
Toowoomba *Town* Australia 91 F13
Topeka *State capital* Kansas, USA 27 D13
Toronto *Province capital* Ontario, Canada 29 J11
Torun *Town* Poland 57 D8
Tottori *Town* Japan 82 G7
Touba *Town* Senegal 64 F3
Toubkal, Mount Morocco 63 E2
Toulon *Town* France 47 H10
Toulouse *Town* France 46 G7
Tournai *Town* Belgium 50 E4
Tours *Town* France 47 D8
Townsville *Town* Australia 91 D11

Toyama *Town* Japan 83 F8
Toyota *Town* Japan 83 G8
Trabzon *Town* Turkey 73 C12
Transnistria *State* Moldova 58 H6
Transylvanian Alps Romania 55 E9
Trapani *Town* Sicily, Italy 48 H6
Trencin *Town* Slovakia 56 I7
Trent *River* England, UK 41 G10
Trento *Town* Italy 48 B6
Trenton *State capital* New Jersey, USA 21 G12
Treviso *Town* Italy 48 B6
Trier *Town* Germany 50 G6
Trieste *Town* Italy 48 B7
Trincomalee *Town* Sri Lanka 77 I9
Trinidad and Tobago *Country* 35
Tripoli *Capital* Libya 63 E8
Tripoli *Town* Lebanon 73 G10
Trivandrum *See* Thiruvananthapuram
Trnava *Town* Slovakia 56 I7
Trois-Rivières *Town* Quebec, Canada 29 I12
Troll (Norway) *RS* Antarctica 16 C4
Tromsø *Town* Norway 43 B8
Trondheim *Town* Norway 42 E6
Troy *Town* New York, USA 21 E12
Troyes *Town* France 47 C10
Trujillo *Town* Peru 36 C5
Tshikapa *Town* DRC 68 E7
Tubruq *Town* Libya 63 E11
Tucson *Town* Arizona, USA 27 G8
Tuguegarao *Town* Philippines 79 E10
Tula *Town* Russian Fed. 58 G7
Tulcea *Town* Romania 55 E13
Tulsa *Town* Oklahoma, USA 27 E13
Tunis *Capital* Tunisia 62 D7
Tunisia *Country* 62
Tunja *Town* Colombia 35 G8
Turin *Town* Italy 48 B4
Turkana, Lake Kenya 67 F9
Turkey *Country* 73
Turkmenabat *Town* Turkmenistan 86 J3
Turkmenistan *Country* 86
Turks and Caicos Islands *Dep. territory* UK 35 B9
Turku *Town* Finland 43 G9
Tuvalu *Country* 93 I12
Tuxtla Gutiérrez *Town* Mexico 31 I12
Tuz, Lake Turkey 73 D8
Tuzla *Town* Bosnia and Herz. 49 C9
Tver *Town* Russian Fed. 58 F7
Twin Falls *Town* Idaho, USA 24 H6
Tyler *Town* Texas, USA 27 G14
Tyrrhenian Sea 48 G6

Uberaba *Town* Brazil 37 E10

Uberlândia *Town* Brazil 37 D10
Ubon Ratchathani *Town* Thailand 78 G5
Uchiura Bay Japan 83 C10
Udaipur *Town* India 77 E8
Udine *Town* Italy 48 B7
Udon Thani *Town* Thailand 78 F4
Uele *River* DRC 69 C9
Ufa *Town* Russian Fed. 59 G10
Uganda *Country* 67
Ukhta *Town* Russian Fed. 59 D9
Ukraine *Country* 58
Ulaanbaatar *Capital* Mongolia 85 C9
Ulaangom *Town* Mongolia 84 C7
Ulan-Ude *Town* Russian Fed. 86 H7
Ulm *Town* Germany 51 I9
Umeå *Town* Sweden 43 E8
Umtata *Town* South Africa 69 J8
Ungava Peninsula Quebec, Canada 29 F11
United Arab Emirates (UAE) *Country* 75
Uppsala *Town* Sweden 43 G8
Ural Mountains Russian Fed. 59 F10, 86 G2
Uruguay *Country* 37
Urumqi *Town* China 84 D6
Usak *Town* Turkey 72 D6
Ushuaia *Town* Argentina 36 J7
Usol'ye-Sibirskoye *Town* Russian Fed. 86 H6
Ust'Ilimsk *Town* Russian Fed. 86 G6
Ústí nad Labem *Town* Czech Republic 56 G5
Ustyurt Plateau Uzbekistan 86 I2
Utah *State* USA 27
Utica *Town* New York, USA 21 E11
Utrecht *Town* Netherlands 50 D6
Utsunomiya *Town* Japan 83 F10
Uzbekistan *Country* 86

Vaal *River* South Africa 69 I9
Vaasa *Town* Finland 43 E9
Vadodara *Town* India 76 E7
Vadsø *Town* Norway 43 A10
Vaduz *Capital* Liechtenstein 52 F5
Valdivia *Town* Chile 36 H6
Valdosta *Town* Georgia, USA 23 F10
Valence *Town* France 47 G10
Valencia, Gulf of 45 F11
Valencia *Town* Spain 45 F11
Valencia *Town* Venezuela 35 F10
Valladolid *Town* Spain 45 D8
Valletta *Capital* Malta 48 I7
Valparaíso *Capital* Chile 36 G6
Van *Town* Turkey 73 D13
Vancouver *Town* British Columbia, Canada 28 I6

Vancouver Island British Columbia, Canada 28 H5
Vantaa *Town* Finland 43 G10
Vanuatu *Country* 93 I12
Varanasi *Town* India 77 E10
Varna *Town* Bulgaria 55 H13
Västerås *Town* Sweden 43 G8
Vatican City *Country* 48
Växjö *Town* Sweden 42 I7
Venezuela *Country* 35
Venice, Gulf of 48 C7
Venice *Town* Italy 48 C6
Veracruz *Town* Mexico 31 H10
Verkhoyanskiy Mountains Russian Fed. 87 F9
Vermont *State* USA 21
Verona *Town* Italy 48 B6
Versailles *Town* France 47 C9
Verviers *Town* Belgium 50 F6
Viareggio *Town* Italy 48 D5
Vicenza *Town* Italy 48 B6
Victoria, Lake Kenya/Tanzania/ Uganda 67 G8
Victoria *Province capital* British Columbia, Canada 28 I6
Victoria *State* Australia 91
Victoria *Capital* Seychelles 69 D14
Victoria Falls Zimbabwe 69 G8
Victoria Island Canada 17 E8, 29 E8
Vidin *Town* Bulgaria 55 G9
Vienna *Capital* Austria 40 E13
Vientiane *Capital* Laos 78 F4
Vietnam *Country* 78
Vigo *Town* Spain 44 C5
Vijayawada *Town* India 77 G9
Villach *Town* Austria 40 H10
Villahermosa *Town* Mexico 31 H12
Villavicencio *Town* Colombia 35 H8
Vilnius *Capital* Lithuania 58 G5
Vina del Mar *Town* Chile 36 G6
Vineland *Town* New Jersey, USA 21 G12
Vinh *Town* Vietnam 78 F5
Virginia *State* USA 23
Virginia Beach *Town* Virginia, USA 23 B12
Virgin Islands *Dep. territory* UK 35 D11
Virgin Islands *Dep. territory* USA 35 D11
Vishakhapatnam *Town* India 77 G10
Vitoria *Town* Brazil 37 E11
Vitória-Gasteiz *Town* Spain 45 B9
Vitsyebsk *Town* Belarus 58 F6
Vladikavkaz *Town* Russian Fed. 59 I8
Vladivostok *Town* Russian Fed. 87 I9
Vlissingen *Town* Netherlands 50 D5
Vlorë *Town* Albania 49 F10

Volga *River* Russian Fed. 59 F8
Volgograd *Town* Russian Fed. 59 H8
Vólos *Town* Greece 49 G11
Volta, Lake Ghana 64 I7
Vorkuta *Town* Russian Fed. 59 C11, 86 E3
Voronezh *Town* Russian Fed. 58 G7
Vosges Mountains France 47 D11
Voss *Town* Norway 42 F5
Vostok (Russian Federation) *RS* Antarctica 16 F5
Vratsa *Town* Bulgaria 55 H9
Vyborg *Town* Russian Fed. 58 E6

Waal *River* Netherlands 50 D6
Waco *Town* Texas, USA 27 H13
Waddenzee *Sea* Netherlands 50 B7
Wadi Halfa *Town* Sudan 66 A7
Wad Medani *Town* Sudan 67 C8
Wagga Wagga *Town* Australia 91 H11
Wakayama *Town* Japan 82 H7
Wakkanai *Town* Japan 83 A10
Walbrzych *Town* Poland 56 F6
Wales *Country* UK 41
Wallis and Futuna *Dep. territory* France 93 I13
Walvis Bay *Town* Namibia 68 H6
Wandel Sea 17 G11
Warren *Town* Michigan, USA 20 F8
Warsaw *Capital* Poland 57 E10
Washington, Mount USA 21 D12
Washington *State* USA 24
Washington D.C. *Capital* USA 21 H11
Waterford *Town* Republic of Ireland 40 H6
Waterloo *Town* Iowa, USA 20 G4
Watertown *Town* New York, USA 21 E10
Wau *Town* Sudan 66 E7
Weddell Sea 16 D2
Weimar *Town* Germany 51 F10
Wellington *Capital* New Zealand 93 F9
Wels *Town* Austria 40 E10
Wenzhou *Town* China 85 G12
West Bank *Disputed region* Near East 73 H9
Western Australia *State* Australia 90
Western Ghats *Mountain range* India 76 F7
Western Sahara *Territory* 64
West Palm Beach *Town* Florida, USA 23 I12
West Virginia *State* USA 21
Whitehorse *Province capital* Yukon Territory, Canada 28 F5
White Nile *River* Sudan 67 D8
White Sea 58 D7

Whitney, Mount California, USA 26 D5
Wichita *Town* Kansas, USA 27 E13
Wichita Falls *Town* Texas, USA 27 F12
Wieliczka *Town* Poland 57 G9
Wiener Neustadt *Town* Austria 40 F13
Wiesbaden *Town* Germany 51 G8
Wilhelmshaven *Town* Germany 51 C8
Wilkes Land Antarctica 16 G6
Williston *Town* N Dakota, USA 25 E11
Wilmington *Town* Delaware, USA 21 G11
Wilmington *Town* N Carolina, USA 23 D12
Windhoek *Capital* Namibia 68 H7
Windsor *Town* Ontario, Canada 29 J11
Winnipeg *Province capital* Manitoba, Canada 29 I9
Winston-Salem *Town* N Carolina, USA 23 C10
Winterthur *Town* Switzerland 52 F4
Wisconsin *State* USA 20
Wloclawek *Town* Poland 57 D8
Wolfsberg *Town* Austria 40 H11
Wolfsburg *Town* Germany 51 D10
Wollongong *Town* Australia 91 H12
Wonsan *Town* North Korea 85 D13
Worcester *Town* Massachusetts, USA 21 E13
Worms *Town* Germany 51 G8
Wroclaw *Town* Poland 56 F7
Wuhan *Town* China 85 G11
Wuppertal *Town* Germany 50 E7
Würzburg *Town* Germany 51 G9
Wyoming *State* USA 25

Xiamen *Town* China 85 H12
Xi'an *Town* China 85 F10
Xining *Town* China 85 F8
Xuzhou *Town* China 85 F11
Yakima *Town* Washington, USA 24 E4
Yakutsk *Town* Russian Fed. 87 F9
Yambol *Town* Bulgaria 55 I12
Yamoussoukro *Capital* Côte d'Ivoire 64 I6
Yanbu *Town* Saudi Arabia 74 F5
Yangon (Rangoon) *Town* Burma (Myanmar) 78 G2
Yantai *Town* China 85 E12
Yaoundé *Capital* Cameroon 68 C5
Yaroslavl *Town* Russian Fed. 58 F7
Yazd *Town* Iran 75 D9

Yekaterinburg *Town* Russian Fed. 86 G3
Yellowknife *Province capital* Northwest Territories, Canada 28 F7
Yellow Sea 85 E12
Yemen *Country* 75
Yenisey *River* Russian Fed. 86 F5
Yerevan *Capital* Armenia 59 J8
Yinchuan *Town* China 85 E9
Yining *Town* China 84 D5
Yokohama *Town* Japan 83 G10
Yonago *Town* Japan 82 G7
York *Town* England, UK 41 F9
Youngstown *Town* Ohio, USA 21 G9
Yucatán Peninsula Mexico 31 G13
Yukon *River* Alaska, USA 25 B10
Yukon Territory *Province* Canada 28
Yuma *Town* Arizona, USA 26 G6
Yumen *Town* China 85 E8
Yuzhno-Sakhalinsk *Town* Russian Fed. 87 I10
Zadar *Town* Croatia 49 D8
Zagreb *Capital* Croatia 49 B8
Zagros Mountains Iran 75 C8
Zahedan *Town* Iran 75 D11
Zajecar *Town* Serbia 49 D11
Zambezi *River* Southern Africa 69 G8
Zambia *Country* 69
Zamboanga *Town* Philippines 79 H11
Zamora *Town* Spain 44 D7
Zanzibar *Town* Tanzania 67 I9
Zanzibar Island Tanzania 67 I10
Zaporizhzhya *Town* Ukraine 58 H7
Zaria *Town* Nigeria 65 H10
Zeebrugge *Town* Belgium 50 E4
Zenica *Town* Bosnia and Herz. 49 C9
Zhangjiakou *Town* China 85 E11
Zhanjiang *Town* China 85 I11
Zhengzhou *Town* China 85 F11
Zhezkazgan *Town* Kazakhstan 86 I3
Zhongshan (China) *RS* Antarctica 16 E7
Zibo *Town* China 85 E11
Zielona Gora *Town* Poland 56 E6
Zilina *Town* Slovakia 57 H8
Zimbabwe *Country* 69
Zinder *Town* Niger 65 G10
Zlin *Town* Czech Republic 56 H7
Zomba *Town* Malawi 69 F10
Zonguldak *Town* Turkey 73 B8
Zrenjanin *Town* Serbia 49 C10
Zug *Town* Switzerland 52 F4
Zürich *Town* Switzerland 52 F4
Zwettl Stadt *Town* Austria 40 D12
Zwickau *Town* Germany 51 F11
Zwolle *Town* Netherlands 50 C7

Index

Acknowledgements

The publishers would like to thank Richard Burgess for his contribution to this book.

All other artworks are from the Miles Kelly Artwork Bank.

The publishers would like to thank the following source for the use of their photographs:

Fotolia.com 10(b) Andrey Mirzoyants, Jean Luc Bohin, Giovanni Catalani, Kárpáti Gábor, Matt Ireland; 20 David Ruderman; 22 Daren Whitaker; 25 Sascha Burkard; 27 Tomasz Kawka; 28 Melissa Schalke; 29 Roman Krochuk; 30 Beatrice Preve; 31(t) Lein De Leon; 34 Françoise Bro; 35 pixphoto; 36(t) urbanhearts; 41(b) C J Photography; 43 Marco Regalia; 44 Hugues Argence; 48 Dubravko Grakalic; 50 Jarno Gonzalez/Fotolia.com; 51 Philip Lange; 52(t) Renato Francia; 54(b) Jozsef Szasz-fabian; 56(b) Bartlomiej Kwieciszewski; 57 Martin Džumela; 58(b) Salazkin Vladimir; 59 Jacek Malipan 65(t) Natasha Owen; 74(t) Richard Connors, (b) MaxFX; 79(c) Dmitry Ersler; 80 Stuart Taylor; 81(b) TAOLMOR/; 83(t) Anna Cseresnjes; 87(b) NFive; 91 Flavia Bottazzini; 92(b) Rico Leffanta; 93 Adam Booth

All other photographs are from: Corel, digitalSTOCK, digitalvision, istock.com, John Foxx, PhotoAlto, PhotoDisc, PhotoEssentials, PhotoPro, Stockbyte

Every effort has been made to acknowledge the source and copyright holder of each picture.
Miles Kelly Publishing apologises for any unintentional errors or omissions.